"*Sisters-in-Law* is the bluebook for practicing law a[...]u through the underbelly of the legal system in [...]e inside scoop on the characters and scenarios a Sister is likely to encounter in practice...along with Sisterly neuroses, obsessions and disorders that we all have, but don't like to talk about. Any woman who has ever had a job, a relationship, or indeed a friend who is an attorney, will read it and laugh out loud."

—Lori Hernando, In-House Attorney, Pfizer, Inc.

"With twenty-five years in both private and government practice, from single and svelte to married with three kids, a dog, a cat, and a sports nut for a boss...I have lived the life the Sisters described. How reassuring it is to know that Sisterhood is NOT a myth!"

—Leslie K. Berg, Trial Attorney, Office of the United States Trustee

"I've been an attorney for over thirty-five years and have worked with many women. *Sisters-in-Law*, with truth and wit, deals with the many issues females confront daily in a system built around male values. It should be requisite reading not only for lawyers, but for all persons in the workplace, regardless of gender."

—Howard Weitzman, Entertainment and Trial Attorney and partner
Proskaver Rose

"FUNNY, INFORMATIVE AND UTTERLY IRREVERENT! The lawyer's mouthpiece for the legal experience, complete with real-life office antics, acres of advice, and honest reassurance neophyte lawyers will find nowhere else. I wish this book was available when I started law practice!"

—Karen Koenig, Of Counsel, Paul, Hastings, Janofsky & Walker

"A MUST READ...Loaded with wisdom, candor, insight and laugh-out-loud humor, *Sisters-in-Law* sets the standard in the legal profession for aspiring and practicing female lawyers, as well as, their male counterparts."

—Robert Shapiro, Criminal Attorney and partner
Christensen, Miller, Fink, Jacobs, Glaser, Weil & Shapiro

"If I ever elect to become a woman, *Sisters-in-Law* will be my bible. Beneath the humor and playfulness of this book are thought provoking insights into the balancing act that all professional women inevitably confront. And for any working man, *Sisters-in-Law* should be required reading."

Sisters -in- Law

an uncensored guide for women practicing law in the real world

Lisa G. Sherman
Deborah L. Turchiano
Jill R. Schecter

SPHINX® PUBLISHING
AN IMPRINT OF SOURCEBOOKS, INC.®
NAPERVILLE, ILLINOIS
www.SphinxLegal.com

Copyright © 2004 by Lisa G. Sherman and Deborah L. Turchiano
Cover and internal design © 2004 by Sourcebooks, Inc.
Cover images © 2004 by Photodisc

All rights reserved. No part of this book may be reproduced in any form or by any electronic or mechanical means including information storage and retrieval systems—except in the case of brief quotations embodied in critical articles or reviews—without permission in writing from its publisher, Sourcebooks, Inc.® Purchasers of the book are granted a license to use the forms contained herein for their own personal use. No claim of copyright is made in any government form reproduced herein.

First Edition: 2004

Published by: **Sphinx® Publishing, An Imprint of Sourcebooks, Inc.®**

Naperville Office
P. O. Box 4410
Naperville, Illinois 60567-4410
630-961-3900
Fax: 630-961-2168
www.sourcebooks.com
www.SphinxLegal.com

This publication is designed to provide accurate and authoritative information in regard to the subject matter covered. It is sold with the understanding that the publisher is not engaged in rendering legal, accounting, or other professional service. If legal advice or other expert assistance is required, the services of a competent professional person should be sought.

From a Declaration of Principles Jointly Adopted by a Committee of the American Bar Association and a Committee of Publishers and Associations

This product is not a substitute for legal advice.

Disclaimer required by Texas statutes.

Library of Congress Cataloging-in-Publication Data
Sherman, Lisa G.
  Sisters-in-law : an uncensored guide for women practicing law in the real world / by Lisa G. Sherman, Deborah L. Turchiano, and Jill R. Schecter.-- 1st ed.
    p. cm.
  ISBN 1-57248-378-4 (pbk. : alk. paper)
  1. Women lawyers--United States. 2. Practice of law--United States. I. Turchiano, Deborah L. II. Schecter, Jill R. III. Title.
  KF299.W6S53 2004
  340'.023'73--dc22
                                                            2004012782

Printed and bound in the United States of America.
ED — 10 9 8 7 6 5 4 3 2 1

Dedication

This book is dedicated to the following **Sisters-in-Law** who sadly perished in the September 11, 2001 terrorist attacks:

Kristen Christophe	VP Risk Services—AON Corporation
Carol Demitz	Chief Corporate Lawyer— Fiduciary Trust
Arlene Fried	VP & Assistant General Counsel— Cantor Fitzgerald
Linda Gronlund	Environmental Compliance Officer—BMW
Barbara Olsen	Political Commentator & Author
Clarin Siegel Schwartz	Senior VP Tax Law— AON Corporation
Joanne Weil	Associate—Harris Beach, LLP

Acknowledgements

I would like to thank Gregory Kamer, my Saintly Mentor, for nurturing me when I had no idea what I was doing; Howard Knee, my Ostrich and favorite ASS, for giving me years worth of material for this book; my Binging and Bitching buddies, who talked me out of leaving the **Sisterhood** to open a flower shop many times; and my support system, most notably, Sari, Karen K., Kim, Jamie and Tali, each of whom share my ongoing battle against LASS and the **Sisterly**-induced disorders. I wish to pay special tribute to my parents who brought me into this world and, despite threatening otherwise, have not taken me out; Geri and Jim, for launching this book in the Sherman over-the-top party tradition; my two beautiful daughters, Alex & Amanda, for sharpening my cross-examination and deposition skills everyday and for making my life full; and last, but not least, my loveable, sport-o-phyle Y-Factor, Jeff—who remains devoted to me, despite never having won a single argument, and with no realistic prospects to do so in the future.

—*LGS*

I pay special homage to my parents, who told me not to go to law school knowing that I would do the opposite of whatever they told me to do; my big drooly-dog Henry, who was the only person who stayed up with me till the wee hours of the night while I drafted this book and binged on raw cookie-dough (his motivations being completely transparent); my daughter, Caprice (nothing to do with the "arbitrary and capricious" standard of law, by the way), who gratuitously provided only the best fodder for pregnancy and working-mommy anecdotes; and last, but most notably not least, the only man who can comprehend and match my sardonic wit—my muse and HINDS patient, Rich—who married me despite my **Sisterly**-induced neurosis and allowed me to borrow his last name for purposes of writing this book only.

—*DLT*

I am grateful to my husband, Dan, who continues to fight the fight in a household full of women—his guidance and patience make everything possible; my family and friends, for understanding that my ability to rationalize anything, especially when it comes to retail therapy, is simply a by-product of my legal education; and, my two Sisters, Lisa and Deb, for magically transforming the most humdrum lawyerly materials into mirthful prose.

—JRS

This masterpiece would still be sitting on someone's windowsill waiting to be filed (*i.e.*, tossed) but for the help and guidance offered by Dianne, Mike, Christine and others at Sphinx/Sourcebooks, who took a chance on this book and actually believed us when we told them that writing about law could be somewhat amusing. We express our gratitude to Eric Sherman and Sarah Sobel for giving us legal advice because *we don't do that kind of law*. Finally, we thank the hundreds of Sisters out there who agreed to tell us their stories without billing us— don't worry, we won't charge you for the free Bitchin' therapy either.

Lisa G. Sherman
Deborah L. Turchiano
Jill R. Schecter
August, 2004

Contents

PART I: BREAKING IN THE PERFECT PAIR OF SHOES:
SETTLING INTO SISTERHOOD

    The Stilettos: The Full-Service Law Firm

    Comfortable Platform Heels: The Mid-Sized Law Firm

    Ski Boots: The Highly-Specialized, Boutique Law Firm

    Orthopedic Shoes: The 9-to-5, In-House Counsel Gig

    Mary Janes: Government Gigs

    Rollerblades: Hang-A-Shingle Shop

    Getting Off on the Wrong Foot

PART III: ONE, TWO, BUCKLE MY SHOE:
EVERYTHING THEY DON'T TEACH SISTERS
IN LAW SCHOOL ABOUT PRACTICING LAW

Preface

—why we wrote this book—

everyone craves more information about the colorful and sexy lives led by female attorneys. But, truth be told, most of us are a far cry from Ally McBeal (both in our day-to-day practice and our suit size). Most female lawyers we have encountered over our collective thirty years of practice are not at all passionate about practicing law, and if they had to do it all over again, they would have chosen a career in *ANYTHING* else—we're talking folding sweaters at the GAP, arranging floral bouquets, bagging groceries...you name it.

The women who have experienced the highest levels of dissatisfaction, many of whom lacked mentors and real-life work experiences, blindly plunged into practice thinking they would be the next Ellenor from *The Practice*. Not knowing how to swim with the sharks (*i.e.,* crazy partners, obnoxious opposition, and demanding clients) or manage their time effectively, their recreational activities outside of *the law* became limited to complaining about their jobs to just about anyone who would listen. Frustrated with the institutionalized process that they never learned to understand and manipulate, they soured, and in some cases, abandoned the practice of law completely.

Against this backdrop we set out to write a practice guide that would give aspiring and newly practicing lawyers, as well as unhappy practitioners, substantive and technical advice on how to succeed at practicing law. When it came to throwing our fellow femme-lawyers a life vest, however, we kept falling asleep on the manuscript because it was so damn boring. With the endless editing, redrafting, and bantering among your authors, each of whom always thought she was right, the text suddenly flew off the page the second we employed our most charming weapon—humor. Through our own colorful experiences and those of hundreds of our colleagues (all of whom love to complain), we set out to expose what it is really like in the trenches as a woman, the inside scoop on the characters and scenarios a **Sister** is likely to encounter, as well as the neuroses, obsessions, and disorders (unavoidable byproducts of the profession) that we all have, but don't like to talk about.

For all you nonlawyers who were kind of enough to buy our book to help us with our nasty *Neiman Marcus* habit, this book is not lost on you. If you have ever worked anywhere before, you will relate to many of our experiences, particularly those related to female office-antics. Our nonlawyer friends (yes, we have some) who read earlier versions of the manuscript reported that they felt the strongest connection with our chapters on interviewing (Chapter 2), the cast of characters in the office (Chapter 4), food and fat (Chapter 5), dating (Chapter 6), pregnancy (Chapter 7), and de-stressing (Chapter 8). After reading the rest of the book, we think you will have a better understanding of the eccentric subculture in which we live and why we tend to be anal-retentive perfectionists who always think we are right.

For those of you who have already begun to practice or have abandoned the field, this book will serve as your trip down memory lane.

You will laugh at the countless scenarios that you have probably encountered at some point in your legal career. You will take comfort in the fact that the neurosis and obsessions that you have experienced during your practice are shared by one and all. Above all, we hope that you learn something from this book that you didn't already know—even if it has nothing to do with practicing law.

Introduction

Step away from the computer, put down your latte, and cease and desist from whatever you are doing. Unsure of whether to go to law school? Uncertain what to do with your $100,000 law degree? Feeling insecure, inefficient, and ill-at-ease at your law job? Welcome to the **Sisters-in-Law** club. Members of the club include, but are not limited to (a favorite *cover your ass* (CYA) legal disclaimer in case you left something out), women considering a career in law, currently enrolled in law school, and current or former practitioners. Anyone who falls within the definition of **Sisters-in-Law** is automatically a member—no registration fees, bar examinations, or moral aptitude tests required.

The problem with joining the **Sisterhood** is that you are generally unprepared for the journey that follows. There is no internship, residency, or procedures manual. And don't think you'll learn anything that prepares you for practice in law school. In law, you learn by doing. Period. The problem is, it's impossible to do when you don't know what you're doing. That's where we come in. We and countless other **Sisters** who have blazed the trail before you are here to equip you with some of the tools, untold secrets, and proper mind sets that you will need to master the art of practicing law and maintaining your sanity.

Using an experience to which all women can relate, we have analogized practicing law to a woman's never-ending search for the perfect pair of shoes. (Admittedly, it gets to be annoying after the first chapter, but it works from time to time.) You want to find the best fit without sacrificing style. You want something that is versatile—fun and unique, yet stimulating—a pair that won't bore you after one season. Once you find your perfect fit, you want to break them in and strut them all around town. (Of course, if it turns out the shoe doesn't fit as magically as Cinderella's glass slipper, off you go to repeat the whole bloody process of finding the right fit all over again.)

So kick back and join us for an uncensored tour through the underbelly of the legal world. Since, like most Sisters, our attention span with respect to everything non work-related is no more than that of a five year old, we have divided this book into three parts. In Part I, *Breaking in the Perfect Pair of Shoes: Settling into Sisterhood*, we guide you through choosing the right scene to practice law, using your feminine prowess to secure the perfect legal position, preparing for your first few days of Sisterhood, and sizing up the cast of characters with whom you will work.

Once you get through this semi-substantive stuff, we toss you some brain candy fluff in Part II, *Footloose and Fancy Free: Having a Life as a Sister*, in which we discuss neuroses that are byproducts of our profession. Specifically, we explore our disorders with respect to food, fat, dating, pregnancy, and searching for a life outside the firm. We will also analyze the meeting of our two worlds: Sisterhood and Motherhood.

In Part III, *One, Two, Buckle My Shoe: Everything They Don't Teach Sisters in Law School about Practicing Law*, we return to the substantive stuff and provide you with a painless primer on the nuts and bolts of practicing law—what it's like to be a litigator, transactional lawyer, general practitioner, or specialist, and of course, making the escape to greener pastures if your current job is not the right fit.

One last point before you read on. This book is written in lawyerese—for those of you who are practitioners, you won't even notice it because you're brainwashed to write this way. For the rest of you, this means that we use:

- long sentences;
- redundant adjectives and phrases to explain the same thing;
- oodles of defined terms and acronyms to save space (which have been provided for your convenience in Appendices A and B);
- Latin phrases because they make us sound smart;
- long, run-on endnotes and cute bubbles filled with useless, but interesting information that doesn't belong in the text;
- long parentheticals when we think something is more than endnote-worthy, but not that important; and,
- annoying bullet lists like this one to provide long laundry lists of trivia.

Get used to it, this is par for the course.

If only finding the perfect pair of shoes were so simple...

Part 1

Breaking In the Perfect Pair of Shoes: Settling into Sisterhood

Sizing Up Your Solemate

-where to practice law-

It's all about choosing the right scene, **Sisters**. Think location, location, location. A three-bedroom house next to the freeway is worth far less than the same house built on a tree-lined street in Beverly Hills. So why doesn't everyone live in Tinseltown? For the same reason only a small percentage of **Sisters** devote their careers to working at large law firms. The cost of a luxurious lifestyle is steep. You must be willing to sacrifice leisure for loot, pride for perks, and ego for eternal servitude.

How do you determine the location best suited for you? Most **Sisters** begin their legal careers in one of the following six settings:

(1) the *crème de la crème*, full-service law firm;

(2) the lifestyle-loving, mid-size law firm;

(3) the highly-specialized, boutique law firm;

(4) the 9-to-5, in-house counsel position;

(5) the benefit-driven, government gig—from the district attorneys' office to a state or federal clerkship; or,

(6) the hang-a-shingle shop.

Join us for an in-depth tutorial on sizing up your solemate.

THE STILETTOS: THE FULL-SERVICE LAW FIRM

Large law firms are the *stilettos* of law practice. Sexy and stylish, these razor-sharp heels can make the most shapeless calf muscles appear taut. These exorbitant, adorned stilts change the posture, gait, and demeanor of anyone who dares to wear them. Don't be fooled, though—behind the illusion you'll find big firm tortured souls whimpering and whining after prolonged wear. If and when, however, a big-firm Sister wants to cast her stilettos away and rest her tired tootsies, the big firm experience will serve as a springboard to bigger and better (or in many cases, kinder and gentler) opportunities.

Almost thirty percent of lawyers nationwide are women, with almost half of them joining the ranks of large law firms after law school.[1] Yet, we would be remiss if we didn't warn you that women account for only sixteen percent of law partners in major law firms nationwide.[2] While the survival rate is oftentimes not much longer than those of suede shoes in the rain, Sisters will continue to do their residencies in the large firm trenches.

The members of these large firms are an elite group—and they won't let you forget it. Entry is frequently limited to those who hail from first-rate schools or who have highly influential connections. Call them *The Four Seasons* of law practice, with top-notch accommodations, state-of-the-art equipment, highly-trained support staff to service every need, and first-class amenities.

Located in the best part of town, these firms pay top dollar to house their prized stallions. Help is available 24/7 on all ministerial matters, like duplication, word-processing, faxing, and car services. Full-time librarians can be called in a pinch to help find the *golden ticket case* (which oftentimes, of course, does not exist). As if this weren't enticing enough, paralegals are stationed close by to provide air and ground support, especially during dangerous operations. If a computer problem is detected at mission control, teams of nerdy Bill Gates prodigies storm the halls to repair and recover a damaged hard drive or important documents. There's always one crisis or another in the big firms, so they keep an over-abundance of staff in reserve to put out the fires at all times.

Big firms operate profitably by hiring large groups of young associates—anticipating attrition before the masses gain too much seniority. We state the obvious when we point out that the more bodies available to work, the more likely you can avoid, or at least minimize, working for poisonous personalities.

There are also the infamous perks of big firm life. In an ostensible effort to promote good physical health (while ironically ignoring mental health), these institutions will often foot expensive gym memberships (typically unused) or, at the best firms, maintain in-house gyms that provide blah gray sweats adorned with firm logos for emergency work-outs. Who ever dreamed a law firm would provide first-class showers, blow-dryers, and toiletries to freshen up?

During crunch times, you will call the office your home away from home. All meals consumed on the clock are provided by the firm. With so little time for self-indulgences, big firm lawyers take the free-meal gig very seriously.

Sidebar

Take, for example, the infamous sushi memo.[3] The story goes like this: A *Sister* partner, who apparently ate undesirable take-out sushi, asked one of her underlings to prepare a memo researching the best after-hours sushi delivery joints. After exhaustively interviewing lawyers and staff members and reading reviews, the underling presented a three-page diatribe complete with eight footnotes and two exhibits (two take-out menus, of course) to the partner. It should be noted that when this memorandum hit the press, the question everyone asked was not *what's the best sushi*, but rather, *whom do you think was billed for this project?*[4]

But don't be fooled, **Sisters**—like everything else in life, nothing comes without a price.

Billing-machine associates will typically log in more than 2400 hours a year. To help you with the math (didn't we all go to law school to get away from the math?), that means an average of 200 hours a month, which is approximately 10 hours a day if you don't work weekends (which you will). If you back out time for bitching, binging, and Internet shopping (on a modest day totaling a good 5 hours), this means that you will be physically at the firm for 15 hours a day! Not much time left to your day, **Sister** (although admittedly, long hours tend to breed steamy office romances, exciting eating escapades, and friendships that will last a lifetime).

We must point out that although you won't be receiving a membership card, you will in fact feel like you have joined a union if you choose to work at a big firm. You see, in most major cities, the law firms generally adhere to a lock-step compensation scheme[5] where, much like *Local Plumbers 181*, you are paid based on your seniority rather than your talent (admittedly, for many of us, this can be a good thing). In fact, at the big firms, your salary and any subsequent increases over the next seven or eight years are set in stone, and one and all have access to this information.[6] Theoretically, everyone works hard and the reward for hard work is partnership, so there's no reason to set differential pay levels. As you can imagine, this makes for quite a few free riders since only 16% of an incoming associate class will ever actually make partner.

Why has a system so lacking in meritocracy survived all these years? The answer seems to be threefold: First, the lockstep system prevents Type A associates from inflicting serious bodily harm on each other because nobody fights over how big a slice of pie he or she is getting. Second, it discourages associates from padding their billable hours in order to achieve a bigger paycheck. Lastly, and perhaps most importantly, the lock-step method benefits Management (the senior associates and/or partners serving as your supervisors).

They are deathly afraid of giving the union members straight-up performance reviews or feedback. When compensation is not linked to performance, management can avoid this dirty deed.

So, why are there are no shortages of candidates willing to amputate their left arm to work in these pressure cookers? It's all about showing off, **Sister**. Large law firms are status symbols, no different from Ferragamo shoes or a Harvard degree. Even more importantly, after laboring for thirty-six plus excruciatingly painful hours to bring you into this world, your mother wants pay back. Nothing will be more satisfying to mommy-dearest than bragging to all of her maj jhong friends that her daughter is a Skadden[7] pedigree lawyer.

At some point you are going to ask: *Is wearing the stilettos worth sacrificing everything else in your life?* For most **Sisters** the answer is, *in the short run—yes; in the long run—no.* If you put in your time at the prestigious name brand firm for a few years, the training and résumé filler are invaluable. You will have the opportunity to work with all sorts of personalities and observe a countless array of practicing styles. More importantly, because these firms are so big, you can fly under the radar when you are having an off day. And for all the heartache, at least you will travel to exotic vacation spots (even if you only see the four corners of a conference room there) and feast on mouth-watering meals at the most expensive restaurants (even if you have to talk shop). Of preeminent significance, the sweat shops will facilitate your indulgences in the latest high-priced fashions (even if you only wear them during the second shift). The big firms pay the big bucks, and **Sisters**, do not underestimate the power of retail therapy.

COMFORTABLE PLATFORM HEELS:
THE MID-SIZED LAW FIRM

Mid-sized law firms are the comfortable, platform heels of law practice. These chunky mid-stacked shoes are in ample supply and won't break your pocketbook. Although clunky and ordinary, these heels provide ample support for Sisters of all weights and sizes, minimizing the risk of embarrassing wipe-outs. Best of all, prolonged wear has no known deleterious long-term effects.

Ranging anywhere from 15–100 lawyers, these firms may value lifestyle as much as they value hard work. Membership is not exclusive. Anyone with a J.D. degree is eligible. These lifestyle-loving law practices are the panacea for the suffering souls from a big firm.

Mid-sized firms eliminate costly and unnecessary luxuries, including expensive office space, top of the line equipment, staff, librarians, paralegals, and last but certainly not least, entertainment. Operating on a bare bones budget, attorneys at these firms have the added pressure of dealing with ministerial nightmares, such as computer crashes and filing mishaps—time that, unfortunately, is not billable to anything but a Sister's social life.

Although Sisters at these mid-sized firms do not sport fancy Ferraris and generally can't swing expensive summer-shares in the Hamptons, they have a life outside work, which is far more valuable to them. While billing continues to measure their worth, the requirements are usually more sensible and, in many cases, relaxed. While all-nighters, late nights, and weekend work are the exception—not the rule—they do occur, but only when truly warranted.

Want to know the best part of wearing the comfy heel? With so little time to administer the firm, management keeps bureaucratic red tape to a minimum and petty administrative matters are glossed over or simply ignored.

On the downside (gosh, aren't we always bursting your bubble?), don't deceive yourself—practicing law is still practicing law. Obnoxious opposing counsel do not disappear and your workload does not diminish into thin air just because you choose to hang your shingle on a smaller post. With fewer attorneys staffing cases, your blood pressure will typically increase in direct proportion to the additional workload. It is also highly likely that in your young and tender years, you could get stuck working with the annoying personalities whose cases the more experienced associates will not take. Unfortunately, you can run, but you just can't hide, from the truly evil partners at the mid-sized firms.

Our assessment? Mid-sized firms are all about finding the right fit. If you were stranded on a deserted island, could you survive with ALL the personalities in the place? If you can't stand the inhabitants, send out the SOS and hop to another island.

SKI BOOTS:
THE HIGHLY-SPECIALIZED, BOUTIQUE LAW FIRM

Highly-specialized, boutique law firms are the ski boots of law practice. Complex and costly, these colorful casts are only used for one purpose. Typically, these lawyers—refugees from the big firms—are rebelling against their roots. To lure the big-fish clients, the boutique specialists sell themselves as big firm lawyers giving more personal attention at bargain basement billing prices. Our advice? There's something to be said for knowing a lot about a little, especially if it's something you enjoy. With tight quarters and small budgets, however, one bad personality will sink the entire ship.

ORTHOPEDIC SHOES:
THE 9-TO-5, IN-HOUSE COUNSEL GIG

In-house counsel gigs are the orthopedic shoes of practicing law. Padded and protected, with unlimited wear and tear, these shoes may not be pretty, but can be a kinder and gentler way to practice law. Usually, however, most **Sisters** must first wear the stilettos or at least the platform heels before they can slip into the comfort of the orthopedics.

For years, many lawyers fantasized about the day they would give their two-week notice to the big firm Muckety-Mucks and take refuge in the perfect in-house position. No billable hours, excellent benefits, only one client to appease, 9-to-5 hours, and the authority to farm out all litigation and deal issues to outside counsel—what could be better?

We are sorry to report, however, **Sisters**, that with skyrocketing litigation and deal costs, many corporations have now moved litigation and much of the corporate work in-house. All of the lawyers who left the throes of crazy deadlines and excessive paperwork must now handle everything, in addition to all of their full-time, day-to-day responsibilities to employees of the corporation. All this for a meager salary compared to the generous compensation at the revenue-generating law firms.

As if their plates were not already overflowing, these lawyers must also play the in-house politics game by contending with the antics of coworkers, many of whom are not lawyers and thus lack the ethics typically held by Newbie associates in a law firm. Managers will take credit for your work and may even play colleagues against each other. Gone are the lock-step compensation increases along with the innocuous nonmerit based titles of *1st year, 2nd year, 3rd year*, etc.

Sidebar

Truth be told, there's a huge upside to working with nonattorneys—your law degree will buy you the highest level of respect in the company, even if you know very little about what you're doing. Apparently, there's something about getting through law school and passing a bar exam that leaves even rocket-scientist nonattorneys in awe. So, give yourself a pat on the back for landing the highly sought after in-house gig, and don't EVER let them think you don't know the answer to something!

While the top players are easily identifiable, the rest of the hierarchy is fuzzy. All of the players share one common goal—to claw their way to the top. Turnover and promotions are few and far between. Again, the personalities are the biggest hazards of the game.

If you can get the in-house gig, however, there are still distinct advantages. Company lawyers overwhelming report satisfaction with their jobs, stemming largely from being part of a team and the close working relationship they share with their client.

From what we gather from our Sister reports, there is a time and place for the in-house gig, most notably when it comes to having bambinos. For whatever reason (but probably due to lack of billables), corporations tend to have better maternity and time-sharing policies than law firms.

MARY JANES: GOVERNMENT GIGS

Remember Mary Janes, your first pair of fancy shoes? These classic shoes were appropriate for every occasion, whether they were scuffed up or shiny new. The government gigs, from district attorneys' offices to a federal court clerkship, are the Mary Janes of law practice—great benefits, flexible hours, mentoring, training, and a less competitive environment. While the digs aren't even on par with a *Motel 8*, much less *The Four Seasons* big firm, the practice and accompanying lifestyle may be well worth the shoddier office space.

Government's Guardian Angels

While it all may sound well and good to put the bad guys away, Sister prosecutors disappointingly report that the justice system is sometimes anything but just. Unfortunately, there is so much crime in the world that the cases must move along like meat on a conveyer belt. Like everything in life, mistakes will happen. Because most crimes are unwitnessed or witnessed by people who have serious baggage, sometimes the bad guys (or gals) are set free. Although you may not single-handedly make the world a better place, it's still the best place to get firsthand experience trying cases.

Defenders of the *Wrongfully* Accused

Even public defenders do not claim that all of their clients are innocent. It's about making sure the system works and the government plays by the rules. Talk about fodder for interesting cocktail chatter and honing trial skills. Just don't go into too much detail with your mother about your client base, and whatever you do, NEVER give out your home number!

Playing God

If you love to research and write, and dream of walking in Ruth Bader Ginsburg's shoes (figuratively speaking, of course), here's your chance. A clerkship gives you the power to play God without the perks. These top-of-the-class, brainiac Sisters are given the power to rule on important matters about which they know little to nothing. The alarming part is that most of them have not practiced law a day in their lives! While the atmosphere is typically more laid back and the hours a dream, the only route to feeding your Jimmy Choos addiction is winning the lottery or getting a generous birthday gift from grandma.

The relationship Sisters develop with their judges is almost universally the best part of the job—your judge is oftentimes your mentor and your friend for life. You will also learn all of the courthouse gossip and get firsthand experience about how the system works. You will observe the process—many times alarmingly arbitrary—in which decisions are made. And let us not forget clerking's greatest (and perhaps most entertaining from a geekoid perspective) feature—you will come face-to-face with some of the worst legal writing, reasoning, and presentations that you have ever seen by members of the bar. Talk about a stroke to your own legal ego!

The downside? Although it will vary depending on the level of the court and on your judge, clerking can become extremely cyclical and monotonous. For those of you who loath change, this can be a blessing, but for those Sisters who are constantly on the go, the routine will seem as exciting as watching grass grow. Fortunately, the judges must have figured this one out by now as most clerkships are limited to one to two years. Career clerks tend to be older types who typically want to do the part-time mommy gig.

Although you will be exposed to a wide array of people while court is in session, the rest of your days will be spent in the equivalent of a 2-foot by 2-foot jail cell. Stranded in a back room researching away, you are only interrupted by an occasional exchange with your judge, an assistant, or perhaps one or two other law clerks. To avoid being placed in solitary confinement, you had better make sure you get along with everyone in your cell block.

Our advice? If you can swing it financially and have the grades or credentials to land a prestigious clerkship, it's well worth it, even if you're not planning on litigating. If for nothing else, a clerkship will enable you to put off the real world for yet another year.

ROLLERBLADES: HANG-A-SHINGLE SHOP

We save for last the footgear that is perhaps the hardest, and definitely the least likely option to be worn by Newbie Sisters—the rollerblades. Imagine heading straight down Mount Everest all alone in rollerblades hopelessly out of control with no protection. Solos' lives are roller coasters (depending what walks in the door on any given day), both emotionally and physically. Typically (but not always), the solo practitioner is the Sister who achieved low to mediocre grades in law school, interviews poorly, or, for reasons unknown, couldn't get a job working for someone else. They are the real cowgirls of law—most of the time they just don't know what they're doing, so they resort to what they know best—winging it. Unless you are independently wealthy, your banker (who approves your credit line) will be your new best friend. With limited access to research materials and office supplies, you will put in long hours playing the part of lawyer, secretary, paralegal, runner, photocopier, office manager, and accountant. Because you will be skating out of control, you must maintain oodles of insurance coverage because chances are, malpractice will be committed as frequently as a newborn baby poops.

Ironically, despite these initial hurdles (and representing the dregs of society), these ladies eventually seem to make the most money over time. Hundreds of petty felonies, run-of-the mill divorces, or small personal injury cases that a large law firm would never touch adds up, especially if you don't have to split the $\frac{1}{3}$ contingency fee (typically, the lawyer's share of the recovery or value of a case) with anyone else! And let us not forget the best parts—you don't have to deal with ANY of the distasteful characters described in Chapter 4; no one will destroy your work or self-esteem (other than your client, opposition, judge, and family); and best of all, if you want to work at home naked, no one will stop you. You are the master of your domain. The only person you have to answer to is yourself.

Our assessment—if you can stomach the unknown in the beginning and don't mind learning and burning, strap on a set of blades. However, to avoid spinning your wheels in the young and tender years, we would recommend renting office space with other (hopefully, more experienced) solo practitioners who may know the answers to your stupid questions (or at the very least share resources and *Reese's* peanut butter cups with you in your moment of need).

GETTING OFF ON THE WRONG FOOT

How many times have you bought shoes that felt perfect in the store and hurt like hell the second you wore them out of your house? While you may be able to suffer through one evening wearing uncomfortable shoes, submitting yourself to torture 24/7 on an ongoing basis is pain few can bear. So, before getting sucked in, think long and hard about your ultimate professional and personal goals. Although every experience in life makes you stronger, you may want to consider starting out with the shoes best suited for your feet, instead of trying to do damage recovery with a proper fit down the road.

If we can pass on one word of experienced advice, it is this—even if you discover that your preliminary path is not quite right for you, your unsuitable initial decision should not be viewed as an insurmountable problem. Some of the most successful **Sisters** have changed their shoes—both in their substantive practice of law as well as where they practiced law—many times in their careers. In fact, many report that never in their wildest dreams did they think they would wind up doing what they are doing today. If you're unhappy, just remember—you are armed with a law degree that opens up endless doors, so don't ever feel hopelessly bound by your current servitude.

■ ■ ■

2

Picking Out the Perfect Pair of Shoes

-securing your first legal position-

Sisters, even if you've never interviewed for a job before, rest assured you have been honing your interview skills for years while playing the dating game. You remember it like yesterday—and for many of you, it was. Before every first date, you obsessed over what you should wear, what you should say, and how you should act. After exchanging initial niceties, you quickly won over your date by laughing at his jokes (however stupid), complimenting his attire (however outdated), and agreeing with his views (however sexist). After some subtle cross-examining in regards to his past baggage and testing the authenticity of his *lines*, if you succeeded, he left wanting more. You then carefully considered the pros and cons of the potential suitor and either decided to pursue the relationship further or rejected him forever.

The fine art of interviewing is no different. You want to leave the interviewers wanting more of you, while at the same time reserving your right to choose among suitors. So, whether you're facing this task for the first time or you're back for a refresher course,[8] we are here to chat with you about how you can use your God-given, superior, feminine powers to find the right home for your new shoes.

You can't expect love at first sight if you answer the door for a blind date in sweats and wet hair. Similarly, there's no excuse for showing up to an interview unprepared. Obtain information about the office and interviewers through law school placement offices or publications such as the *Vault Report*, *American Lawyer*, and good old Mr. Hubble (Martindale, that is). The National Association of Law Placement (NALP) keeps statistics for particular offices of law firms, which is helpful in determining practice areas and demographics. Most importantly, though, you are now blessed with the holy grails of research—the World Wide Web and Saint Google—so you can pull all sorts of interesting tidbits about a legal employer and its lawyers online.

If you know enough about what the office has to offer, you will appear knowledgeable, confident, and calm (despite the fact that the butterflies in your tummy have morphed into rabid bats). There are few things more embarrassing to a candidate—and more irritating to an interviewer—than expressing a profound interest in ERISA law, only to find out too late that the office only practices Admiralty law (okay, extreme example of peculiar practices, but you get the picture).

One cautionary word about research—be discreet. If you're lucky enough to know with whom you'll be interviewing beforehand, and you learn other than obvious details about him or her, use your insider information wisely. You will give the interviewer the heebie-jeebies if you bring up intimate details about his or her wild college days.

QUESTIONS

While not every interview is the same, there are some fundamental lob questions you should be prepared to return. You'll likely hear one or more of the following insipid queries.

Our favorite response—"I had a botched nose-job when I was 13. If it had not been for the excellent advice and counsel of my parents' medical malpractice attorney, I may still have had that lop-sided shnoz today. Since then, I have wanted to go to law school."

WHY DID YOU GO TO LAW SCHOOL?

Let's face it, many of us would simply reply *college was over*. You don't have to intern for the President of the United States (although we question whether this is a marketable credential anymore) to formulate a stellar response. Just connect your motivation to a tangible and sincere explanation based on prior experiences in your life.

WHY ARE YOU INTERESTED IN WORKING AT OUR LAW OFFICE?

Of course, the interviewer is probably asking himself the same question. You must fight the uncontrollable urge to respond *because you pay the big bucks*. Instead, grab on to something you learned from your research and tie it into your interests.

WHAT DID YOU DO LAST SUMMER?

If you've had a law-related experience, exploit it. Any solid explanation of what you accomplished (besides catching up on the complete second season of *Sex and the City*) will score points, even if the interviewer knows you were just partying on the summer associate bandwagon.

WHAT ARE YOUR WEAKNESSES?

The number one answer of **Sisters** surveyed is *chocolate*. While this is guaranteed to loosen up your audience (unless they have no sense of humor), you still have to answer the question. Be prepared to spin like a disingenuous top—turn weaknesses into strengths.

Our best response? "I don't know how to say 'no' because I always aim to please." Since everyone is looking for a chump for a legal dump (*i.e.*, passing on horrible assignments to junior associates), you can bet this response will get you the job (along with everyone else's drudge-work).

WHAT DO YOU LIKE TO DO IN YOUR SPARE TIME?

Although no one expects you to have volunteered with Mother Theresa in Calcutta (although it wouldn't hurt), your interviewers are looking for you to tell them something interesting and unique about yourself that has nothing to do with the law. Be creative, and, dare we say it, consider the *Law Interview Embellishing* (LIE) technique.

Sidebar

One **Sister**, who grew up with a Westhighland Terrier used to play hairdresser with her dog. Years later, utilizing the LIE technique, she put the pictures in a portfolio and boasted to interviewers about her entrepreneurial dog grooming business. Not only did she land the legal job, but she was so convincing that the interviewer made a date for her Maltese on the spot!

You should also be prepared to address any questions about geographical desirability. If you have no discernable connections to the city, your chances of an offer are slim to none. If you have spent your whole life in Chicago, you must be able to explain to an L.A. employer that your desire to spend the rest of your adult life in the city is based on more than watching *Baywatch* (not that any **Sister** would ever watch that show). For example, if one of the puppies from your dog's litter was adopted by a family in the Hollywood Hills, you may consider utilizing the my entire extended family lives in the area LIE.

If you forget everything else we tell you, just remember to sell yourself and say something interesting. The worst thing you can do is leave an interviewer wondering how he or she can get those last fifteen minutes (or .25 hours) of time back.

We'll let you in on a little secret—there are only three reasons busy lawyers volunteer to do interviews. First, if you receive an offer, recruiting attorneys get to pick the Zagat Top-50 restaurant for the good old *wine and dine* routine. In other words, you are their meal ticket. Second, some firms count recruiting time towards billable hour requirements and interviewing is less painful than researching. Lastly, horny male associates like to pull for the hotties, no matter how qualified (from a legal perspective) these **Sisters** may or may not be.

SPEED DATING: THE SCREENING INTERVIEW

The screening interview is really just speed dating, but arguably with more at stake. The interviewee will meet with about twenty candidates all in the same day, one smack right after the other. All of the candidates probably have impressive credentials, and all are trying to win the interviewer's heart to score the sacred call to come back to the firm to get drilled by the rest of the crew (the *call-back*).

In reality, the screening interview is generally a mere formality. The real decisions are made on the basis of the candidate's resume and transcript, which have been received ahead of time. In other words, the interviewer just wants to make sure you don't have three heads (even if you had three heads, you would be protected by the *Americans with Disabilities Act* (ADA), and the employer could be sued if they did not give you a call-back on this basis).

If you fall somewhere in the middle like the rest of us, your fifteen minutes in the hot seat may make a difference, so you must be prepared to shine. Go with the flow of the conversation, but don't feel compelled to spend the whole time discussing the Rule Against Perpetuities.

Sidebar

For non-**Sisters**, the Rule Against Perpetuities is an esoteric Property Law theory that everyone spends an entire semester trying to understand, but no one really ever grasps. In fact, the bar exam preparatory class instructors explicitly tell you that you stand a better chance to get the Rule Against Perpetuities question right by filling in the *B* bubble than actually thinking through the question.

Nonlaw related accomplishments that you didn't think were exciting may in fact make you stand out. For example, one **Sister** reported that during her interview with a male partner, she casually mentioned that she had worked the previous summer at ESPN. Since most guys would give their left [insert any body part you can think of] to be on a first name basis with any woman who has any connection to the four letters *ESPN*, this **Sister** instantly made the call-back cut. (Funny thing was, she had only been a temporary file clerk for ESPN.)

THE DATE THAT NEVER ENDS: THE CALL-BACK INTERVIEW

This phase is all about endurance. At a smaller office, you may be scheduled for a rigorous morning or afternoon of back-to-back interviews with several different attorneys in the pecking order. At the larger law firms, the call-back is often an all-day affair, with scheduled meetings throughout, a lunch with several associates, and perhaps even a dinner. At a government office, you may be sequestered into a windowless room the size of a port-a-potty while three district attorneys bombard you with unanswerable hypotheticals.

Irrespective of the schedule, the goal is the same and the end result is pure exhaustion. You have made the cut on paper at this point and all that is left is the fit. The associates will want to know whether you are a person with whom they can play *Trivial Pursuit* at 2 a.m. at the printer and the partners will try to figure out if your cost is worth your benefit (*i.e.*, the revenues you generate in billables will be equal to or exceed four times your salary).

Take a look at whether the secretaries appear to be happy and relaxed (even when they are not on ciggie-break). Usually, there's a *funnel-down* effect from the top, so if the staff is generally happy, the associates are probably treated with respect and will generally be happy too.

You, of course, need to play Karen Sisco[9] and feel out the office culture. Although you have no assurances that anyone will give you the real scoop about what it's really like to work there, you should look for the subtle hints and clues right in front of your eyes. For example, do people avoid eye contact in the hallways or look as if they are sleepwalking?

During the call-back, you will typically meet with about four or five attorneys, one right after the other, with no time to breathe. Realize that everyone at the office has his or her place in the food chain and it's more important to impress the whales than charm the minnows. If your interview with three junior associates goes fabulously, but in your interview with the partner, you mispronounce the firm's name, you're history. Conversely, if the partner loves you but you tell all the other associates with whom you interview that you're not available to work after 5 p.m., you don't do weekends, and, by the way, this firm sucks, you're still golden.

This process takes at least three hours, so by the end of it all, you feel like it's the morning after a rave party (not that we've ever been to one, but from what we've heard). Your voice is hoarse from bragging about yourself, your mouth is dry and hurts from fake smiling, you're famished, you have a killer headache, and your short-term memory is shot. By the third interview, you will probably stop listening to what the interviewer is saying and start thinking about what you're going to order for lunch. At the very least, be mindful not to ask the exact same insipid question more than once.

After lunch, you will usually meet once again with Julie McCoy (the recruiting director). She will ask you if you have any other questions and, just like your date at the end of a so-so evening, promises to be in contact *soon*. If the employer wants you, *soon* usually means that night via phone or within a week in the mail. If the employer is on the fence about you and wants to extend offers to all the kids from Harvard before it sees if it has enough room for little old you, *soon* may be by the end of the recruiting season. If the employer thinks that you may be better suited to practice law in a cave in Afghanistan, it's possible that *soon* could mean *never*.

■ ■ ■

3

Preparing for Sisterhood
in Your New Shoes

-surviving the first week-

So now you're a big shot with a job in your back pocket (hopefully of a nice little pair of Sevens that you have rewarded yourself with for getting an offer). Even if you held the honorable position of summer associate at your new residence, you are now faced with the reality that the annual summer charade,[10] has come to a screeching halt. To start off on the right foot, you will need to overcome your *prework* jitters, get up to speed on the basics, and understand all of the silly little cultural eccentricities that will soon be your norm. So, without further ado, permit us to join you in your first steps in your new shoes.

THE OFFICE MAKEOVER

Before we can properly advise you on how to make your office warm and fuzzy, we need to address the real estate issue. If you're lucky, you'll get your own housing accommodations. If you happen to be in a big city where real estate is expensive and you overhear the recruiting director say on more than one occasion *oops, we made too many offers*, you will be stuck with a roommate. And we use this term literally. You can bet your Manolos that the person sharing the tiny 10 x 10 cube will know you better than you know yourself. So, to prevent petty spats, try your hardest to make your new roommate a Bingin' and Bitchin' Buddy, your new best friend and confidant, with whom you do everything, most notably binge and bitch.

If you are stuck sharing, usually the only way that you can claim your own abode is the magic A-word—attrition. Of course, a **Sister** would never wish death or serious disability upon any of her fellow associates to get a better office, but her *evil twin* **Sister** knows that for every associate that kicks the dust (usually due to defection to another law firm rather than death), one more person on the single-or-better office waiting list will have her Christmas wish come true.

While we're talking about real estate, the value of your property decreases in proportion to the proximity of certain unsavory partners and annoying associates. Unless you are the suck-up attorney we know you are not, living next door to the *paparazzi* (lawyers who monitor your comings and goings and live to tell other people about them) is never a good thing.

You might also say *there goes Mr. Rogers' neighborhood* when a yeller or screamer moves close by. This character will make trying to concentrate at your desk a living hell because long, loud, and annoying conference calls will never be made with the office door closed. He or she also yells out tasks for the secretary instead of paging, calling, or, God forbid, getting up and going to his or her desk. If you actually get a choice of offices, we would suggest selecting that prime real estate situated on the *Escape from Alcatraz Route*, but not too much of a shlep to your secretary or the loo.

Escape from Alcatraz Route— The shortest route from your workspace to the elevator/entranceway measured in time and distance.

So, how do you make the most of your tiny, dingy office that in all likelihood was formerly used as the due diligence file overflow room? No reason to keep this *fee simple*.

Although there's a slim chance of achieving *Feng Shui*, let us guide you on how to make your office a more pleasant space to toil away.

Fee simple—for those of you who are lawyers, you have to love that foreign language we spent days trying to comprehend in Property class. Just about as useful as learning Swahili. For all of you aspiring Sisters, fee simple is Property-ese for an interest in real estate.

Wall Art

In most jurisdictions, you will proudly hang your diplomas on the wall across from your desk. They remind you that no matter how stupid and clueless you may feel from time to time, at least one state and board of bar examiners believe that you are worth over $150 per hour. There is one glaring exception to this rule. At the big firms in New York City, hanging any kind of qualification document is considered gauche and taboo—after all, wasn't everyone at the firm on law review at Harvard or Yale?

If you work at one of these shops or if you'd rather keep it a secret that you graduated from law school before some of the paralegals were born, consider hanging other serene and tasteful pieces of artwork. For those of us not blessed with a hole to the outside world, hang a picture that looks like something you may see if you had a window.

If you have children and you want to show the world how gifted your offspring are, most Sisters have no qualms about displaying a few pieces of kiddie-art. We especially like those stick-figure family pictures that always make Mommy look very skinny.

Desktop Goodies

Display pictures of family members, animals, friends, and perhaps your boy toy to inspire you in times of need (so long as he does not make you hot and bothered). We probably don't need to tell you this, but don't leave anything valuable in your office. Typically, no one sweats the small stuff, but the second someone's Zagat guide is declared missing, an all-out sting operation is launched.[11]

Many **Sisters** also keep a candy dish on their desk to lure in visitors and make new friends. Trouble is, most of this candy will inevitably be eaten by yours truly during a moment of weakness (which occurs no less than thirty times a day), so we suggest filling it with a something that you detest (like those leftover black jellybeans from Easter). The funny thing is, even when you fill the jar with the pink marshmallow candy that you thought nobody would eat, people will continue to stop by and devour it simply because it's free.

Desk Drawer Goodies

Three words—Keep Emergency Supplies. This includes: tampons, sanitary pads, extra hose, extra pair of underwear for any kind of strange and unexpected accidents, nail file, clear nail polish (for nails and rips in hose), tweezers (**Sisters** typically obsess about errant facial hair more than commas or periods), toothpaste, toothbrush, deodorant, Tylenol/Motrin/Advil, prescriptions, and most importantly, chocolate. In other words, pack up your desk drawer like a weekend suitcase because you may have more than one unexpected layover in the office.

Speaking of your drawers, let's hope you have enough room for the shoe drawer. Most **Sisters** report they have one of these babies exclusively reserved for no fewer than eight pairs at a time, mainly because they want to wear a comfortable pair to work (a necessity if you walk to work, but also helpful to avoid right heel scratches on your Pradas when you drive). These drawers are also helpful if you want to keep your going-out shoes (for after-work dates) or your staying-in slippers (for comfy all-nighters) handy. If you don't have a spare shoe drawer, all of your delicacies will need to be stashed under your desk, and because the cleaning people never bother to pick them up when they vacuum, your shoes will eventually morph into one big shoe-clump mountain under one corner of the back of your desk.

BATTEN DOWN THE HATCHES

Before you start your first assignment, you want to make sure you are fully equipped with all the necessities. To get your ship ready to sail, we suggest the following preparations.

Raid the Supply Cabinet

Remember the days when you were broke and either in law school or studying for the bar, but there was no price you wouldn't pay for the cool multicolored highlighters and sticky-tabs, without which you swear you would have failed? Those days are over, Sister—you've hit the motherload. You are now privy to every pen, pencil, marker, binder, hanging folder, and label color under the sun, along with writing pads, envelopes, and binder separators all of which come in twenty-seven different sizes. It's a virtual anal-retentive orgasm.

Perform a Systems Check

It's not NASA, ladies, but all the electronic gadgets you'll be asked to master will make you feel like you're in Cape Canaveral. In many of the big firms, they will actually have a training session during your first week when the people in charge of computers or the phone department (yes, big firms also pay people a full-time salary to do nothing but deal with phone issues) will tell you everything you need to know, plus more, about these gadgets. Even if your firm provides such sessions, however, the training will usually occur after lunch and chances are you will sleep through it. At a minimum, get your secretary or one of the techie guys to get you up to speed on the following gizmos.

TELEPHONE

Alexander Graham Bell would be so proud to see how we lawyers inexplicably complicated his simple little science project. Making any call is now no longer as simple as a 7-digit input. If you make an internal call, it's just the extension. Outside calls will usually require an extra digit. If you're really lucky you will need to input about 50 digits before going long distance (that's 11 digits for the phone number and approximately 39 digits for the client code numbers). To save approximately two minutes a day (about $17 in billing), you should consider programming frequently called numbers (like your secretary, mother, and Bingin' and Bitchin' Buddies). You should also master redial, speakerphone (to facilitate your Multitasking Madness Disorder), three-way conference calling, and transferring calls within the office. There is nothing more embarrassing than cutting off the Top Brass calling from Hong Kong.

Multitasking Madness Disorder—A disorder that commonly inflicts Sisters who juggle an overwhelming number of personal and professional demands each and every day, making you, out of necessity, a pro at doing several different tasks at once.

There is one feature of the new and improved phone systems that is a curse and a blessing at the same time—caller ID. On one hand, it lets you know when your buddies are calling and it can screen a call from the crazy Associate looking for the State of Nebraska's law—on everything. On the other hand, it precipitates a

Top Brass— The big Muckety-Muck rainmakers in the office.

widely known disease inflicting **Sisters** known as *Partner Paranoia* (the PP's). Within minutes of spotting a call coming in from the dreaded partner, who gave you the PP's by bitching you out for something wholly insignificant, your heart starts racing, you sweat through your silk blouse, and you eat no fewer than fifteen Hershey's kisses to take the edge off of this dire situation. (But we suppose that's better than being surprised by the ballbuster when you pick up the phone.)

VOICEMAIL

Remember Ferris Bueller, the rogue high school student who out-smarted everyone with calculated outgoing messages when he wanted to play hooky? You too can program your outgoing voice-mail message strategically and it will become your screening dream machine. You will also need to learn how to access voicemail both in and out of the office as well as master the basic functions of *forwarding* (to send your assignment to another unsuspecting junior associate), *deleting* (to wipe out your mother's whiny messages for-ever), and *saving* (to listen to the message from that hot guy over and over and over again).

COMPUTER SYSTEM

Strive for expertise on the computer system—it is your electronic lifeline. Yes, we know you have a secretary, but really, unless you were born before 1950, we assume that it's usually easier for you to do your own typing than to write things out for secretarial input. If you want to become more efficient, your secretary can teach you how to operate office macros, format documents, create templates, and play a mean game of solitaire.

FAX/COPY/SCANNER MACHINES

Whatever you do, make sure you get a primer on how to use the firm's fax, copy, and scanner machines. While big firms have their own fax departments (yes, they pay people to do this too), there will be a point in time when you just have to do it yourself. Ditto for the copy and scanner machines.

Even if you master the basics, so much can go wrong: collating, paper sizing, enlarging, toner, and what we all fear the most—ERROR: PAPER JAM. So, while we know you didn't go to law school to make copies—let alone, fix these annoying machines—they're your lifeline, so you better get a tutorial on performing a *paperectomy* and curing other common maladies.[12]

As a side note, while these apparati may resemble office equipment, they are enormous revenue-generating devices. Because clients usually pay huge surcharges for copies and faxes, frequent use of these machines will pay for the partners' kids' private school tuition.

DICTAPHONE

We are aging ourselves when we admit that we lived through the gradual extinction of this ancient artifact. The dictaphone dinosaur is, however, still used by the older lawyers who think the computer on their desk is a dark TV screen. The concept is actually brilliant—babble a lengthy motion into a microphone, have a leisurely lunch, and return to find a perfect product ready for filing. Wake up, Sister—dictating is more often like ordering caviar and ending up with a plate of chopped liver. Something inevitably gets lost in the translation (particularly if you have a Southern accent and your secretary is from Staten Island). Our advice—limit dictation to recording your billable hours, giving instructions to your secretary, or other efficient nonsubstantive matters.

MISSING IN ACTION DEVICES

Some would say that we are now blessed with a garden variety of *Missing in Action* (MIA) devices. From our cell phones, pagers (rather extinct, but some of the old geezers love them), home fax machines, and email to the ability to access your office's network system from home, it's virtually impossible to go AWOL.

Although the MIA devices are essentially a doggie collar, you are on a long retractable leash. Now, instead of waiting at your desk for a client call from Asia after 9 p.m., you can take the call from the changing room of your favorite lingerie store.

Another distinct advantage of the MIA devices is that it will give the appearance that you are at work when you are not. You become Casper, the Friendly Lawyer. We have heard from anonymous sources that you can actually program an email or voicemail to send at some point in the future, preferably in the wee-hours of the morning. No longer must you wait in the office until 4 a.m. to accidentally hit *reply all* to a firm-wide distribution to prove that you're a real trooper. Now you can program your email or voicemail to time stamp while you are home and sound asleep. Simply brilliant!

We would be remiss if we didn't touch on the newest MIA kid on the block, the Blackberry. For those of you who may have been living on a tribal reserve in a third world country, this is the traveling email system. This device is affectionately referred to by users as the Crackberry because once you have it, you can't go without it, and once you check it, you can't stop checking it. Nevertheless, it's here to stay, and will in fact be one of your most trusted friends.

WHY MAGELLAN SHOULD HAVE BEEN A LAWYER

Now that your new office is Sisterized, you will need to map out all of the ingress and egress routes. There are simply too many times when you will need to get from point A to point B and avoid the local stops along the way. So grab the fire escape map posted all over the office (the one that no one ever looks at) and map out each of the following routes.

Escape from Alcatraz Route

The Escape from Alcatraz route is the shortest and most discreet route from your workspace to the elevator or entranceway measured in time and distance. This is the most important route if you need to leave the office early or dash off for a midday interview with an ostensibly kinder, gentler firm.

Dog and Pony Parade Route

The Dog and Pony Parade Route is the scenic route around the office. When you are trying to impress potential clients, new recruits, or family members who don't believe you work, escort them past the most impressive conference rooms and corner offices.

All-Nighter Exercise Route

If you are pulling an all-nighter, chances are you will need to clear your head. After picking up your takeout in the lobby, explore the entire office. It may be beneficial to take note on the All-Nighter Exercise Route which partners' offices have the coziest couch if you need to catch a few zzz's. Beware, however—you will not be the only creature roaming around at night. The early morning cleaning staff is likely to scare the B-Jesus out of you at some point.

Library Route

There are usually several paths to the library (your home away from home in your early years). Analyze them. If there is ANY chance that you will be stopped by either an annoying colleague who will talk your ear off or a partner who might grab you to work on an unwanted assignment, do not pass GO. Select a Library Route that will allow you unfettered direct access. Bring some snacks to the stacks so you don't have to come out for air and risk being discovered.

Bathroom Routes & The Pee-Pee Predicament

In an average day at the office, you will need to use the loo a couple of times. Unless you're one of the annoying *Ally McBeal* characters, this is the one sacred spot off limits to the guys, so use it to sneak in some valuable shmooze time or eavesdrop on the latest gossip.

We would be remiss if we didn't let you in on a well-known, rarely talked about phenomenon called the U-turn. It is when a **Sister** aborts the mission (you turn) the second she sees someone she is working for in there. Most of us would rather risk a bladder infection or an accident than listen to or smell their superior's insides being emptied while discussing the merits of a case.

Unfortunately, sometimes you'll already be doing your business when someone you don't want to see walks into the stall right next to yours. One **Sister** told us that she would always know that her crazy boss had entered the neighboring WC because she could see the partner's Chanel-pointy shoes under the stall wall. Another surefire giveaway that she was within earshot distance was, yes, the sound of her pee. This partner would urinate nonstop, for record periods of time—once up to three minutes straight! (Yes, the **Sister** timed it). Seems that this partner was too busy to take a bathroom break more than once a day. As if that weren't revolting enough, let us not forget to tell you about the third clue. It also seems that this partner was too busy to wash her hands. All right, we'll stop here. This is just way more information than you need to know about anyone, let alone your crazy boss.

But your bathroom worries don't end with the little girl's room. Oftentimes on your way to the loo you may notice the men in your office paying a visit to the little boy's room. You will note that the men, unlike the women, will generally take reading materials to their meetings into the little boy's room. All you can do is hope and pray that these materials are limited to the sports page and do not include your memo, which the guy will invariably hand back to you for edits on his way out after using the urinal. (Eeeeew.)

Although we've provided you some of the necessary office navigation tools, chances are you will have to test the waters and find the path of least resistance. Even then you may encounter some unexpected stops along the way.

SISTERLY TRICKS OF THE TRADE

Now that you have set up your home away from home and figured out the office-maze, your next task is to maximize your efficiency so you can GET OUT at night. From interviews conducted far and wide, the following is a collected list of tips from Sisters to get you started.

Make Lists

You can't imagine how much making lists will help you remember and prioritize your tasks. And when you are on a big case or deal in which you spend hours, days, and even months on internal conference calls, lists will be a lifesaver. Every time an issue or task comes up, it will generously be doled out to you, oh special Newbie associate. To give you an idea of the relative size of lists resulting from these conference calls—they will be much longer than the list of all the guys you've ever slept with (hopefully), but probably shorter than your list of qualifications for a perfect husband.

Calendaring

Let us let you in on a little secret—EVERY Sister has woken up at least one time in her career thinking she blew a big deadline. Unfortunately, system failure is no excuse for the big fat malpractice case that will be brought against you for missing a deadline. As a safety net, double calendar due dates in the office's computerized or more antiquated carbon copy ticklers system and on your own personal calendar/PalmPilot to remind you of critical due dates.

Filing

We're not talking about your nails. You must master the office's method for internal organization of client documents and files. You need to get a primer on how documents theoretically move from your outbox to the proper client file. If your new digs are anything like the rest of ours, however, the filing pile is like your Halloween pumpkin—it sits around on your window sill for months at a time until it simply rots and gets tossed out.

THE ANNUAL BILLATHON

Unless you are employed in-house, most of you will not be fortunate enough to work for an employer who does not use billing as a yardstick for performance. Thus, life as a lawyer will revolve around recording your time billable to clients in tenth or quarter of an hour increments. Most firms will list a *minimum billable requirement* in their recruiting literature, but in reality, you should consider adding the number 1,000 onto that paltry statistic to reach the number they expect from you.

The annual billathon is typically synchronized with the employer's fiscal year. For many firms, the billable year is measured from February 1 to January 31. This means that the entire month of January is high season at Hotel Law Firm, when associates check in but they don't check out in order to rack up their hours. For the month of February (after the completion of the annual billathon), it's like hurricane season—Hotel Law Firm is completely vacant.

In any event, among new lawyers, billing is often an obligation shrouded in mystery, fear, and doubt. Like that jiggly stuff on the back of your thighs, it's pretty impossible to get rid of or ignore the billing regime. Here are some observations to get you thinking about the process.

What You Should be Doing

In an ideal world, your billing ethics will honor and obey the following three commandments.

1. THOU SHALT BILL ONLY FOR THE WORK YOU PERFORM ON BEHALF OF THE CLIENT.

It's almost impossible to research nonstop for ten hours without thinking about sex or, at the very least, food. We are not supposed to make the client pay for our sex or food fantasy breaks.

2. THOU SHALT MAINTAIN CONTEMPORANEOUS TIME RECORDS.

When you start at the firm, the nice recruiting director (whom you will never see again during your tenure) will hand you a pad that has boxes for each tenth of the hour and spaces to fill in for client names and descriptions. These pads are only used in the first week of an associate's life, after which they become kitty-litter lining. However, at the end of each day you should try to scribble down somewhere which clients you worked for and time spent. Just make sure to write it down on a piece of paper that doesn't get folded up into your pockets and subsequently erased forever by your washing machine.

3. THOU SHALT MAINTAIN ACCURATE TIME RECORDS.

You should be keeping a log of detailed descriptions of tasks performed. Gone are the days of *8 hours: prepare and workup case*. Most clients want to know precisely what their lawyers are doing to earn their keep and your billing is supposed to tell the story.

(As an aside, you should also save all backup work even if your research comes up empty. There is nothing worse than having a client question the work and lacking the proof that you actually performed it.)

What (we have heard) Happens in Reality

The problem with billing is that it's impossible for it to be 100% accurate. You simply cannot write down what you are doing every six minutes of the day or you would never get anything done. Attorneys push the envelope on the billing issue to all sorts of extremes, but here are a few cases that even the most ethical attorneys can rationalize.

TRAVEL TIME

This is the best way to rack up the hours. Even if you don't work on the plane, you can generally bill the client for your time spent traveling. In some egregious cases, we have heard of attorneys working on a different client's file so that they can bill double time while traveling. This practice has become taboo since clients got wind of it, but it doesn't stop most **Sisters** from watching the in-flight movie, sleeping, or boozing on the plane instead of working since they can bill for the time anyway.

WAITING TIME

We're not talking the one-hour wait at the doctor's office. We're talking waiting for a client from Europe to call; waiting for a partner to review a memo; waiting for word processing to turn a document; or, waiting for your part of the deal to be negotiated until the wee hours of the night. This excruciatingly painful waiting time is generally caused by partners or clients waiting to review your work until 7 p.m., at which time you're so pissed off that you want to bill triple. As a compromise, you bill your waiting time even if you were playing solitaire.

CREATIVE STORY TELLING

All litigators know that filing day in a big case may be consumed by relatively mundane and menial tasks. Transactional attorneys know that paralegals with a high school education can do most of their work. However, the time sheet description, *copied documents, corrected comma-faults and split-infinitives, saved my secretary from a nervous breakdown, and yelled at the incompetent messenger*, however true, will never fly with the client. Instead, you must highlight the attorney-related tasks, such as: *review, revise, and finalize memo supporting merger; draft documents; conference call with client re: exhibits....*

INNOVATIVE MATH

The general rule of thumb is that if you are at the office for eight hours, you should bill no more than six. However, most Sisters rack up those billable hours using the following technique. If you bill by the ¼ hour and you have four calls with four different clients each less than 15 minutes, you can actually bill more hours than you worked. If you continue to perform different tasks on several different files, the hours will add up quickly.

SELECTIVE MEMORY

If you are working at a ball-busting sweatshop, you will have some crazy stretches of all nighters and long days. You barely have time to brush your teeth, much less record your time. In these cases, most Sisters throw their hands up and surrender, and simply bill 300 hours for the month of February to *working on Fortune 500 deal*. Anyone who questions their integrity after such a horrendous month risks impalement.

Expenses: A Girl's Best Friend

Most Sisters would admit that there's nothing better than some-one else paying for their shopping sprees. Well, you've hit the jackpot if you're working at a big firm for a client who wants the work performed yesterday. If you work through lunch and dinner, the client picks up the tab. If you pull an all-nighter, who do you think pays for those caloric donuts? And there is nothing better than cashing in on mileage reimbursements for the long car rides to court, all of it tax-free!

While you may be thinking that all of these reimbursable items render your firm the closest you'll ever get to a Shuga Daddy, beware. You may be questioned about your reimbursement practices, and it's a silly thing that can mar your reputation. If in doubt, always ask yourself if you can defend the expense to a client with a straight face.

Bitchin' and Billin'

Sisters, if there is one savior to the billable day, it is none other than our favorite therapeutic pastime—bitchin' and billin'. After intense concentration for several hours, take a walk down the hall, plop yourself down in another Sister's office, and start bitching. Topics may range from sexist comments by opposing counsel to dieting and diuretics. It is not only revitalizing—you may even get around to brainstorming legal issues that are billable to the client!

Don't Talk about It

One last tip about billing—stop talking about it! Unless you are venting to your Bingin' and Bitchin' Buddies, it's totally distasteful to ever brag about how many hours you have accumulated for the week, month, or year. By the same token, bragging about all-nighters is for paralegals. You put in the hours, you know how hard you worked, and no one else really cares (except, of course, the partners before they receive their quarterly draws). More importantly, you don't want the person to whom you boast to one-up you!

■ ■ ■

Armed with your colorful digs, electronic expertise, a map of your new world, and an understanding of the annual billathon, let's take a deeper look into the cast of characters you are likely to encounter in your new abode.

4

Familiarizing Yourself with the Shoe Department

-sizing up the cast of characters-

now that you've given your office a makeover, it's time to size up the cast of characters you will be spending more time with than your own family. Oddly enough, they will become like your family. Even the ones you adore will drive you crazy after you have spent too much time with them. And you will find a way to be civil to those you would not befriend if they were the last people on earth, because you all live under the same roof and have to play nice together to get the job done.

You will also soon learn that your first impression of these nice people you met for twenty minutes each was a bit off. While chances are you were probably shielded from meeting the BBQ's (as defined herein) during the interview process, the tyrants that you did meet were on their best behavior during your call-back interview. Even the best of us are misled when it comes to first impressions of lawyers.

Navigating through the office personalities and determining who will pull you up the rungs of the legal ladder can be your key to success. Learn as much as you can about each person in the office. Just because attorneys bear important titles such as partner, shareholder, or vice president does not mean they have the power to order Xerox paper, much less influence your career. Similarly, just because some attorneys have seniority based on their years of practice or their years working at a particular office (and thus higher on the letterhead), does not mean that they wield more power over your paycheck. Just as significantly, you must steer clear of the recluses and sociopaths, as any association with them will be detrimental to your career (and possibly your health).

Brace yourself to join us in a behind-the-scenes look at the motley crew you will encounter during your legal career.

YOUR SUPERIORS

It's all about the money. Different attorneys will simply have different value to you. The key to success is no different from the search for the perfect shoes. Why waste your time and feet on dozens of frumpy pairs? Find those Guccis and Ferragamos and DO NOT LET 'EM GO. Seek out the top of the line and invest your dollars wisely.

There are only so many greenbacks to go around and you can't afford to blow them on a bad investment. Choose the character for whom you work carefully, and perhaps you too, Sister, may be on your way to the corner office.

The Top Brass ($$$$$)

The Top Brass are the big Muckety-Muck rainmakers in the office. Although many of them have not truly practiced law in years and have the legal skills of a first semester law student, the Top Brass make all final decisions, despite their claim that all decision-making is done by consensus. If any member of the Top Brass does not take a liking to you, you are as good as done.

The Ostriches ($$$$$)

Despite their ability to litigate or negotiate a deal ferociously, the Ostrich attorneys are the gangly but loveable birds who bury their heads in the sand when faced with conflict or confrontation outside of their cases and deals. Their poor business acumen is evidenced by their inability to ask clients for retainers, collect from deadbeat clients, and their unwillingness to ever dump a bad apple client. Basically, their hearts are in the right place, but their heads are in the sand. Despite these shortcomings, remember that the Ostriches are great mentors, bosses, lunch mates, and lifelong friends—just don't get into any business ventures with them.

The Closers ($$$$$)

Every office has at least one attorney who is called in to close the deal or charm the pants off members of the jury, judges, or clients. The Closers are always meticulously dressed, tanned, relaxed, and charismatic. Sexual energy and grace somehow exudes from their pores. They are always unprepared and unconcerned because they are accountable to no one. All they need to know on the way to the first day of trial or the deal negotiation are the names of the parties and the end result sought by the clients paying their expensive upkeep bills. Stick close to the Closers and maybe some of their luck will rub off on you.

The Saintly Mentors ($$$$)

Yes, **Sisters**, Saintly Mentors do exist, but they are a rare and endangered breed. How they survived the abuse of the Yellers, Screamers, and Abusers (see page 46) may be the result of large doses of lithium or perhaps just an unnaturally resilient nature. Regardless, you want to find these people and not let them out of your sight. Not only will they help you become a better lawyer, but they will ultimately promote your career (and, if nothing else, let you in on the firm gossip).

The Ball-Busting Ice Queens (BBQs)($$$)

Unfortunately, we all know at least one *Ball-Busting Ice Queen*. These women do not pretend to be your friend, mentor, or champion, and their bark and bite are equally stinging. They resent everything about you and make no bones about it. They will make your life as a **Sister-in-Law** hell so that you too can suffer all of the injustices that they incurred on their way up the ladder. Avoid BBQs at all costs.

The Yellers, Screamers, and Abusers ($$$)

Res ipsa loquitor, **Sister**. Every firm has attorneys whose voice precedes them and they don't care. You will hear them through closed doors. Sometimes you may hear inanimate objects hitting walls. If you have to work for them, your only solace is to commiserate with your fellow colleagues.

Res ipsa loquitor—a latin phrase that means the thing speaks for itself.

The Quiet Terrorists ($$)

These are the quiet senior attorneys who work strange hours in dimly lit offices that resemble pigpens. BEWARE—they are typically walking atomic bombs ready to go postal at any moment.

The Billing Machines ($$)

Every firm has an array of reclusive attorneys who bill all day and all night long. They manage to pull all nighters even when nothing is due and business is slow. Unless the Billing Machine also happens to be a member of the Top Brass, avoid working for or with them. They will expect you to put in the same type of hours as they do, even in the absence of emergency situations.

The Ancient Relics ($)

Many offices have their share of Ancient Relics, usually founders of the organization, who have nowhere else to go except to the office. Their office, the best corner office with a window in the building, is sought after by all attorneys in lesser offices. Oftentimes, for reasons unbeknownst to us, they will be found stalking the conference rooms after everyone has left the meeting, scouring the tables for the leftover cookies. While it is very pathetic, you are responsible for saying good morning, good evening, and checking if their respirator is working and heart is still pumping each day.

The Celebrity ($)

A Celebrity is usually a former governor or senator (or relative of same with political aspirations). He or she has never practiced law, but the firm showcases him to clients and recruits. Paid an annual salary in the six-figure range in exchange for annual billables in the three-figure range, his or her job is to bring in government business, use connections to influence legislation in favor of the firm's clients, and pull strings to get any of the partners out of trouble for dubious conduct. He or she will also do an inordinate amount of high-profile pro bono cases that will buy votes. Not worth your time to kiss up to this character, who will eventually leave the firm to run for another public office. Be polite though. If the race is lost, you can bet he or she will be back.

YOUR COMRADES

Not only must you size up all the attorneys with seniority over you, but you must also size up your fellow attorney classmates. Just like the members of your family, you cannot choose the members of your attorney class. The best you can do is assess the particular characters before the rat race begins. Here are a few personality profiles of your comrades that you are sure to meet in your legal career.

The Teflon Pretty Faces

There is always at least one pretty face who lives under the radar—stress free at all times. Usually, but not always, they are Ivy League graduates with very large trust funds and/or legacies. They arrive late with the paper in hand and seem to do very little throughout the day, except plan their next eating excursion. Work just bounces off of their teflon pretty faces. Buddying up with a Teflon Pretty Face can't hurt you and marrying one of them can only help you.

The Affable Alligators

The Affable Alligators are exactly as they sound—affable to your face at all times, but behind your back they plot your destruction like ferocious alligators who stalk their prey. You will not see them around, except when they try to convince you to go home so that you don't meet your minimum billable hour requirement. They may also try to convince you to work for the most evil attorneys in the office so that they can avoid them.

The Lifers

The Lifers are lifetime senior associates or of-counsel attorneys who have worked at the office for what seems like an eternity. You are likely to hear their longevity statistics touted during your interview to convince you that there is very little turnover. Although the lifers are benign individuals, they are not anyone with whom you want to be closely identified (although if you can visit with them on the DL, they are the best source of historical gossip of the office).

The Ticking Time Bombs

The Ticking Time Bombs are the attorneys whose faces are most likely to be plastered on milk cartons and poster boards every-where under the heading *Wanted: Dead or Alive*. They are typically schizophrenic. They can brownnose the best of the Top Brass while at the same time demonstrating sociopathic tendencies at the wee hours of the morning. Beware of any peculiar behavior and do not say anything more than hello or good-bye to them. In many instances, they will mysteriously disappear from the office never to be seen again.

The Motor Mouths

No matter what time of day or night, the Motor Mouths are the know-it-all attorneys who think they know everything and spend the better part of break times and meal periods arguing esoteric points of law as if they are comparing their penis sizes. (Big sigh.) Take two extra-strength Tylenol and avoid at all costs. Their batteries will run out eventually and hopefully you will be around to observe it.

The Saviors

The Saviors are the attorneys in your class who throw you a life vest each and every time you are drowning. No matter how busy they are, they always have time to help you in times of crisis, to cover for you when you need to get out of a thorny situation, or just hear you vent during those tough days. Find your Saviors and NEVER let them go.

Bingin' and Bitchin' Buddies

Your best friends and confidants, your Bingin' and Bitchin' Buddies are the attorneys you do everything with, most notably binge, binge, binge and bitch, bitch, bitch. Your rendezvous are filled with eating and drinking large quantities of highly caloric food and drinks and complaining about anything and everything. Each day begins with planning your work assignments for the day around your feeding, shopping, and bitching schedule. A typical day consists of a mid-morning walk, followed by lunch, a quick shopping fix, and a late afternoon bitch and Baby Ruth session.

Are you overwhelmed yet? Rest assured, **Sister**, not all of these personalities will work at your office at any one time. However, your new digs are not filled with attorneys alone. No production can happen without a crew of behind-the-scenes players, who in a law firm setting probably wield more influence than, well, you.

THE SUPPORT STAFF

You will learn quickly that despite your seven years of advanced education, you are the lowest rung on the ladder. Not even the janitor is below you. As sad as it is to admit, many of the **Sisters** in the previous generation may have blazed a poisonous trail with the support staff, leaving a bad impression for you to overcome. Before you even think of asking anything of anyone, you need to learn the ropes. There is nothing worse than stepping on the wrong toes. As much as you think that the attorneys in your office will influence your career and help you, the support staff can be just as critical.

The Secretaries

In your first months of practice, think of your secretary as the seeing-eye dog assigned to you. She is that important to your initial blindness in your first months of practice.

If your secretary has been treated like spoiled milk sitting on a grocery shelf, then your job is simple—two minutes a day of chitchat. And while, we know you didn't go to law school to collate documents, a little sorting will allow you to sit on the beach in Hawaii undisturbed. If all else fails, employ your best weapon—bribery.

Before you even finish stashing your chocolate supply in your bottom drawer, you will learn the rank of the secretary assigned to work for you. Generally, they will fall into one of two categories: (1) the Cadillacs, who are sought after by all members of the office or (2) all others, who may be dysfunctional, insecure, disinterested, and/or filled to the rim with 'tude (attitude).

THE CADILLAC

The Cadillac is the premier secretary in the office. Usually described like a Cadillac—runs smooth, efficient, effective, and willing to go the extra mile. Seek out the Cadillac and make overtures towards her each and every day so that you can maximize your chances of trading up in the future.

THE TYPING TERRORS

Almost every office has their share of Typing Terrors with whom attorneys must contend. Their typing skills are excellent, but their attitude is always demoralizing and destructive. Keep those fingers busy typing at all times and minimize social contact.

THE YENTAS

The Yentas are usually older women who have been legal secretaries since the Declaration of Independence was signed and have watched too much *Fiddler on the Roof.* They are overly sweet, nosy, and overbearing—at all times. At first, you may think it is wonderful when they catch simple mistakes, but after they rewrite one too many of your enclosure letters, you will no longer be receptive to their suggestions. If you are a single Sister, it may be time to create a make-believe boyfriend to shield you from their attempts to play matchmaker.

THE UNLICENSED ATTORNEYS

Some secretaries become Unlicensed Attorneys as they engage in the unauthorized practice of law—right down to signing their names on legal documents they prepare. The attorneys for whom they work are phantoms that never make an appearance. Don't worry—they usually know more than the attorneys anyway and you can learn a lot from them if you treat them with respect.

THE CHRONIC HYPOCHONDRIACS

There is nothing worse than the secretaries whose personal problems are too numerous to count. Chronically late to work, the Chronic Hypochondriacs typically take an inordinate number of sick days and are just, how shall we put it, dysfunctional. You can usually find them weeping and whining all day long, seeking attention from whomever will listen, particularly the UPS guy. No sooner will you ask, *How are you?* in the morning than they give you a blow-by-blow saga of the problems they are having in their personal lives. The second you try to interrupt their story with a work-related issue, their demeanor suddenly changes and any and all production comes to a screeching halt. Turn a deaf ear and keep communications to a minimum.

THE PRIMA DONNAS

Having just reached puberty, the Prima Donnas are young girls fresh from legal secretary school or the equivalent, and are easily identifiable. Usually, horny male associates who have no one to stroke their fragile egos will find salvation in these young gals. After a little slapping around, these girls develop from pleasing larvae into bitchy butterflies who refuse to take direction from anyone.

THE JALOPIES

Unfortunately, there are a lot of Jalopies out there. They are dysfunctional, inefficient, ineffective, insecure, unreliable, rebellious, and unwilling to go the distance, let alone the extra mile. Avoid using at all costs and if you do, keep careful tabs on them.

SHARE AND SHARE ALIKE

Unless you are a Top Brass, you will typically be required to share your secretary. While all of us were taught to share and share alike, lawyers are not conditioned to share anything, especially their secretaries. So while you may be required to share your secretary with an attorney senior to you, he or she will not be so inclined to share equally.

UNTOLD SECRETS OF THE SECRETARIAL Sisterhood

What most of you don't know is that legal secretaries are paid well. While they all moan and groan about their compensation packages, they may be among the highest paid individuals in the office. The secretaries who work for Yellers, Screamers, and Abusers and the BBQs usually are given additional combat pay because they are not easily replaceable and they need to be bribed to take such unrewarded grief. The sum of their base salary, combat pay, and bonus often exceeds the annual compensation packages of associate attorneys.

As much as the attorneys complain about their secretaries, they have a symbiotic relationship. For reasons not entirely known, no matter how poorly the secretaries perform, they are not disposed of quickly. The reason for this includes:

- qualified, responsible, and experienced secretaries are an extinct breed and your superiors fear that if they let go of the Jalopy, the replacement will be even worse;
- the cost of replacement and training is high—both in time and money;
- the fear of being sued dissuades attorneys from terminating employees—especially because most of them have witnessed first-hand what plaintiffs collect when they sue their employers; and,
- general apathy. While change can be good, apathy is usually an easier way out.

On the flipside, secretaries, like all employees, need good job references and they too need to put food on their table. No matter how much they like to complain, most of them stay put for years despite their unhappiness. This is because:

- they don't want to go from the frying pan into the fire;
- they like to complain because it is cheaper than therapy;
- there are a few good apples whom they like and who keep them from leaving; and (most significantly),
- general apathy.

THE UNCENSORED SECRETARIAL CLUSTER

In many of the larger firms, your secretary will work together with a pool or cluster of two to three other secretaries. These arrangements are used to assure that you will never be without support. But beware, Sisters—inevitably, one secretary will feel like she is pulling more weight than the others in her cluster. The daily cluster combat antics often provide the best gossip in the office on any given day. Two things to remember:

(1) do not get too wrapped up or engaged in any fights—it will only burn you down the road, especially since the secretary on the opposing side of whatever side you have chosen may in fact be the pet of the Top Brass and

(2) inevitably, it's going to end in a shuffle of secretaries from one cluster to another, tantamount to a transaction as complicated as solving the Rubik's Cube. Our advice? Stay as neutral as Switzerland!

Your Pals, the Paralegals

Think of the paralegals as the nerve-center of the entire operation. While no one wants their job, they make it clear that they are not going to take it from any arrogant attorney. If you bring them into your inner circle, you will be rewarded in more ways than one. They know all the gossip, see all the internal memos, keep all the documents, and most of all, know where all the bones are buried!

While all blame and responsibility ultimately lies with you, if you treat them right, paralegals can organize document-intensive matters and help you with all the menial tasks. Not only will they organize your files, they will type, copy, collate, staple, and prepare exhibits, notebooks, and presentations. They also know how to find and copy cases in the library and online, summarize depositions, and prepare tables and other documents. A good litigation paralegal may even be able to draft discovery requests and responses. A good transactional paralegal can organize all incoming and outgoing deal documents, keep track of all of your schedules and exhibits, and even perform some due diligence.

Somehow, the paralegal has the power to catch any spelling, grammar, or defined term or cross-reference inconsistencies in his or her sleep. This service is critical when you are running on a deadline and don't have the time to check and proof your work a million times. This leaves you, **Sister**, with a beautiful document to review first thing in the morning with your Frappacino and bagel.

And, okay, we know it's outside the scope of their responsibilities, but honestly, there's nothing more that most paralegals love than to get out of the office, even if it means running a menial errand for you.

In our experience, most paralegals will fall within one of two categories.

THE TRANSITIONAL PARA

Typically, the Transitional Paralegals are smart college graduates who either blew the LSAT's, did not apply to any safety law schools, or simply want to put off Socratic madness for another year. They tend to be very organized, diligent, and are genuinely excited about what you are doing. They are happy to help in any way possible.

Socratic method— an annoying teaching technique used in law school where the professor never teaches you anything, but just keeps asking questions.

THE CAREER PARA

The Career Paralegals run the gamut from actors, musicians, artists, and fashion gurus (who repeatedly announce their intent to quit just as soon as they get their big break) to the unmotivated lifers who think they know it all. For some reason (probably due to their longevity), their mental stability and consistency is sometimes called into question. Treat them with the same type of deferential respect that you treat your secretary.

UNTOLD SECRETS ABOUT PARALEGAL COMPENSATION

Most paralegals receive a very poor base salary and can typically double or even triple his or her salary by working overtime. You should never hesitate to ask the para to pull some late hours with you, especially if it entails menial tasks that you should not be doing. Besides, they love bragging to their friends about how much they work.

The Late Night Word Processors

The Late Night Word Processors are generally located down the darkest hallway of the firm, and it takes several journeys to remember where these night owls are placed. There can be anywhere from a handful to two dozen of them sitting desk-by-desk clicking away while simultaneously carrying on three different conversations. They are a wonderful resource if your regular secretary couldn't get your work done during the day or if you finally finished your mark-up at 5 p.m. and your secretary is less than a memory at that point.

In many big firms, you can also take overflow work down to the processing center during the day if your secretary is busy with other work. In general, these people are great at typing and making your document look pretty, but do not rely on them for proofing or any other discretionary tasks. Leave that to the paralegal.

The Rest of the Gang

The help described in this section receive the brunt of the attorneys' wrath. **Sister**, do yourself a favor and give them a few extra minutes and you will be rewarded.

LIBRARIANS

Librarians are only hired by big offices as a luxury. They are usually brilliant attorneys who have some sort of advanced degree in library something or other. Everyone, including the BBQs and the Yellers, Screamers, and Abusers, treats them with the highest respect. The librarians are a good source for trying to research difficult issues, especially when you have no familiarity with the subject matter. Before you start working on your first research assignment, it is a good idea to ask the librarian for a tutorial of the library and secondary sources to make your job easier. If you play your cards right, **Sister**, your book-smart helper can make you shine!

COPIERS

Imagine sitting in a windowless room staring at the bright light of the copier while being chewed out all day long by attorneys who want their duplications finished yesterday. It's as bad as it seems, so if you take those few extra minutes to talk it up with the copy guys, your work will have a faster turnaround.

One **Sister** tells the story that she received a box of documents from opposing counsel and brought the unopened box into the copy room. After turning her charm on full throttle, she asked them to make copies as fast as they could so that she could prepare for her deposition the following day. Halfway through duplicating the documents, one of the copy guys came into her office hesitantly and questioned the origin of the documents. It turned out that the documents were soaked in urine. This **Sister's** relationship with the copy crew was so good that they were willing to copy ½ a box of urine coated documents for her because they did not want to let her down! Thankfully, they didn't contract any diseases, but it certainly demonstrated their loyalty.

INFORMATION SYSTEMS

The IS person is usually a computer geek who speaks in a form of English you cannot understand. When that little bomb appears and everything appears to be lost from your fifty-page brief, this is the person you call in a panic. Make friends with the IS person the first day and seek out their advice to minimize those panic attacks before they happen. Smaller firms often do not have the luxury of having an information systems department to troubleshoot computer problems, but they ordinarily employ at least one secretary who receives the attorneys' wrath when everything is lost. To prevent such disasters, learn as much information as possible about preserving your work.

RUNNERS

Runners are hired to deliver documents from one place to another under stringent conditions. No matter how organized and put together you are, you will cut a deadline close at least one time in your legal career. Most of the time, it is not you, but your bosses, secretaries, or some other unforeseen problem that delays your documents from getting out the door on time. To make sure your runner is moving at his swiftest pace, deliver a periodic bribe and whatever you do, make sure you exchange general pleasantries.

FILE CLERKS

There is nothing more boring than filing documents all day long, updating books in the library, and being chewed out by irritable attorneys and their staff for misplaced papers. All of it falls on the file clerks, even if it is not their fault. For every three bad file clerks, there is usually one good one. Seek them out, make friends, and persuade them to file for you (and while they're at it organize your office and your life). An iced latte can go a long way, Sister.

MAILROOM WORKERS

Anyone willing to work in a law office handling mail after the anthrax attacks deserves a medal, to say the least. These mailroom workers are the first lines of defense against these deadly powders— so remember that before you scream at them while you're waiting for an important letter.

RECEPTIONISTS

The receptionist is the first person to connect you to the outside world. Any messengered items, phone calls, and clients will first come to them, so it is important to act as though you appreciate what they do for you even though (1) you don't and (2) they don't do more than tell you the items or person is at reception. However, as a bonus, if you strike up a good relationship with them, all the conversations they overhear at their desks can be yours.

CLEANING CREW

The same crew usually cleans your office day in and day out, so you will become intimately familiar with them. Usually, when you hear someone walking down the hall in the middle of the night speaking a foreign language, you are relieved to learn it is only the cleaning crew and not the boogie man. Most **Sisters** do not think the cleaning crew does anything more than empty the garbage cans, but a few leftover slices of pizza may get you a dust job, too.

■ ■ ■

As you can see, although your plate will be full kissing up to the big dollar sign attorneys and making nice with your secretary, you may have little time to devote to the rest of the gang. Just remember—a box of chocolates or other sundries at Christmas time will pay you dividends from the rest of the gang all year long.

Speaking of chocolate and vacations, join us for a fun-filled look at food, dating, getting married, pregnancy, motherhood, and striking the right balance between the demands of **Sisterhood** and our desire to maintain a personal life as we move on to Part II.

Part II

Footloose and Fancy Free: Having a Life as a Sister

5

Sisters' Favorite Topic of Conversation

-food, food, and more food-

We know the drill. You were up at the crack of dawn after three slaps at the snooze button, survived a long, grueling day at the office, and staggered home just in time to catch *Friends*—and we're talking about the late night syndicate rerun. It's pretty much you and the entire pint of *Cherry Garcia* on the couch. Although you know that a **Sister** cannot subsist on *Lean Cuisine* alone (mostly because the bird size portions will leave you famished!), who has time or energy for weekday culinary wizardry?

However, most would agree that they live to eat just as much as they eat to live. When we're in the office, nothing gets us more excited than planning feedings with our buddies, rehashing our eating experience, and plotting our next culinary venture. Ironically, after we come home at night, many of us, short on time and energy, limit our foody passion to mediocre takeout or a desperation dip into chocolate chip cookie batter (the kind that comes frozen in the log, of course). Unfortunately, for many busy **Sisters**, the kitchen remains a source of intimidation and the unknown.

This chapter (our favorite, due to the enticing subject matter) takes an in-depth look into a culinary habits in the office and at home. We also provide you with a few quick tips so that you can cultivate your inner-Martha talents (cooking, not stock trading) on a Sister's schedule and budget.

BREAKFAST TO GO

In many firms, breakfast is considered wimpy. Really. You never see any Muckety-Muck lawyers with a poached egg on a lightly toasted croissant on their desk. Instead, the Top Brass choke down black coffee (anywhere from 1-20 cups before noon), no sugar, as a sign of power. So then why did your mother keep telling you that breakfast was the most important meal of the day? Because (argh), she was right.

For many years, one Sister told us that she skipped breakfast, thinking she'd save those precious calories for later. This led to her being famished by the early evening and substituting about 4000 calories in cookies or chips for those 200 calories of Total she would have eaten for breakfast. Admittedly, bingy-food is more fun than breakfast food, but you will need to buy more fat jeans to compensate, and that is no fun. To drive home this point even further, as a general matter, most of the svelte Sisters we know pop something in their mouth before 10 a.m., while the more zaftig ones hold out until lunch.

THERE ARE NO FREE LUNCHES: WORKING MEALS

For many of us, lunch is our favorite meal of the day. It splits the day in half (well, at least for those of us working *part-time* who go home at 6 p.m.) and gives us a chance to mentally and physically recharge for the remainder of the day.

Heed some advice from those who have been in the trenches. Barring work-related emergencies (a legal caveat all lawyers use before committing to social engagements) take the time to break away if you can. As much as you try to avoid it, there will still be

Loosely defined, a Bubble Associate is a lawyer on the brink of partnership. Consequently, this person lives at the office night and day; is a nervous wreck; and, suffers from the most extreme form of kiss-ass syndrome.

plenty of lunches spent at your desk when you don't have time to eat at all. Besides, a hop, skip, and jump down to the firm's lunch-room (although fraught with peril of bumping into the part-ner waiting on your work) always provides the possibility for catching up on local gossip. Nothing leaves you more refreshed and recharged for a pro-ductive afternoon than hearing a lit-tle smut about your coworkers and bitch-ing about the Bubble Associates.

We also recommend against bagging your lunch to pinch pen-nies. Not only will you be the recipient of snide remarks like *don't we pay you enough* (the answer in your head always being *NO!*), but have you inspected the insides of that firm microwave lately? It's like a big lab experiment of old food splatterings, which rivals the cootie population living in the office refrigerator.[13] Trust us, if you choose to look the other way and reheat that leftover pasta, it may look like last night's dinner, but it will taste like last month's pork lo mein, yesterday's burnt popcorn, and today's Hormel chili.[14]

Sidebar

It's possible to derive all the nutrition you need from leftovers in the conference rooms. Take note of the meeting schedule each day and join the other vultures who swoop in and grab as much food as they can carry, just like a sample sale. Of course, this isn't limited to food. Skinny vultures will walk out looking like Humpty Dumpty after stuffing their pockets and mid-section with unopened canned diet colas and bubbly waters.

LETHAL LEGAL SNACKING

As you probably know, the diet-rage *du jour* has been that you should consume multiple snacks and small meals throughout the day. Problem is, these snacks must be limited in caloric intake. We're talking 1 Peppermint Patty, 1 small cookie, half of an apple, or 10 M&M's. Not a chance in hell. Lawyers have a hard time doing anything in moderation, least of which is restricting caloric intake in one sitting. In fact, most of us are like goldfish—we will eat until we explode.

We would be remiss if we didn't warn you ahead of time—before you make a habit of 5,000 calorie snacking while drafting—about a serious malady that afflicts the lawyer population in epidemic proportions within a few months of their start in practicing law—Lawyer Ass Spread Syndrome (the dreaded LASS). Remember the *freshman fifteen*? LASS is like the *first year fifty*, only this time it distributes itself entirely in your butt as a result of spending far too much time in a desk chair. (As a sidenote, LASS afflicts male attorneys just as commonly as us girls, leaving many of the men in your office with a freakishly weird pear-shape physique.) Gravity is not your friend and she just seems to pull all the excess fat down to the hind regions. Worst part is that while everybody else notices, you have to do some pretty limber twisting in the bathroom mirror to monitor the situation closely.

So, in order to help you identify if LASS is knocking at your backdoor (no pun intended), here's some telltale symptoms and our **Sisters'** collected solutions for dealing with it.

Symptom #1 Binge Eating

The need to binge goes something like this: Client needs an answer in one hour. Intercom buzzes. Big Muckety-Muck demands your presence immediately. Tone suspect, length and substance of meeting unknown. What did I screw up on now? Before you have a chance to obsess, the instant messenger displays *URGENT* on your computer screen.

It feels like the walls are caving in and it's only 9:00 a.m. Yoga breathing techniques fail. Your mind is racing. What do you do? You open up your bottom drawer and start digging feverishly like a dog who smells a bone until you get to your hidden stash of.... We're not talking organic carrots, **Sister**.

Symptom #2 Unconscious or Bored Eating

One **Sister** tells of her bright idea to keep a jar of tootsie rolls on her desk to bait the savvy secretaries and friends in for a little mid-afternoon munch. Problem was, when she would work into the wee hours of the night with no one around, fatigue would set in and she would go through the jar of tootsies one by one. Same story with frequent trips for soda, the doughnuts in the lunchroom, and the five-pound ham and brie sandwiches leftover in the conference rooms from client lunches. Office life is littered with chances for unconscious ingesting. You chew, you swallow, you spread.

We're not dieticians here (always a CYA disclaimer with us), but here's our collected thoughts on ways to win the battle of the LASS.

DRINK UP H2O

We're talking an ocean minus the salt. Keep a full glass of water at your desk at all times. Weirdly enough, some big firms even provide you with a water cooler in your office. (We're guessing because you can bill more if you don't dehydrate at 3 a.m.) It fills you up with no calories whatsoever. If you sip throughout the day, you will down the recommended eight eight-ounce glasses with ease. Never mind that you will be in the loo a lot.

Bottom line—*Got H2O?*

SNACK WISELY

Keep lots of nutritious snacks on hand at the office to avoid temptation to eat garbage or to binge to fill the ravished tummy. Nutrition bars are a pretty good staple for the desk drawer, although we would advise against the pure protein ones that taste like moist cocoa saw dust and make your pee green. Not your first choice, we know, but Sisters will do what it takes to avoid the LASS.

GET UP AND MOVE!

Take every opportunity to exercise. Walk down the hall instead of emailing. Take the stairs instead of the elevator. Walk to lunch or work instead of driving.

CHEW LIKE A COW

This one is a last resort for those of us with a serious oral fixation. Keep your desk stocked with sugar free gum and stick a piece in your pie-hole instead of the candy. Although you may sound like the character Fran from the TV show, *The Nanny*, you will note that Ms. Drescher never suffered from LASS.

DINING ON THE HOME FRONT

So why even discuss more than tearing open a box of Pop-Tarts for dinner? Because there is a little bit of Betty Crocker in all of us. You see, cooking provides us with an outlet for our creative talents that were quashed by the rule of law. And the longer you practice, the more you realize that no one will ever admire and compliment you for the seventeen tons of paper you push as much as they do for your homemade apple pie. In fact, many of us get more satisfaction from preparing a perfect roast than writing a perfect brief.

The Cooking Dilemma

Even if you have the culinary bug, many of us are stymied in the kitchen for all sorts of reasons. A **Sister's** cooking excuses basically fall into three Culinary Affirmative Defenses (CAD).

An Affirmative Defense is an excuse or justification for a party's behavior. A *culinary affirmative defense* is an excuse that we use to justify why we don't cook.

CAD #1: I DON'T HAVE THE TIME TO STOCK THE KITCHEN WITH ESSENTIAL INGREDIENTS AND GADGETS, NOR DO I HAVE THE TIME TO SHOP AND PREPARE MEALS.

Let's face it: You are a very busy girl. On any given night, you will probably get home no earlier than 7 p.m. There really isn't any time left to the evening if you want to work out, see your friends, or do anything else for that matter. Cooking does, admittedly, require advanced planning, shopping, and preparation time. In other words, it requires a commitment. While most of us have invested 100% of our bodies and souls in representing our clients (not to mention finding Mr. Right), when it comes to making a date with a ribeye steak on Thursday

Sidebar

As an aside, we want to mention that there is one author who must have an insight into the neurotic mind of a **Sister**. Check out Christopher Kimball's *Cook's Illustrated* Magazine and website:

www.cooksillustrated.com

His *ad nauseum* explanations of how to cook and why things happen (based on several hundred test-precedents) will satisfy even the most anal-retentive **Sister**-cook.

night, we turn into complete commitment-phobes. How do I know if I will be in the mood to eat a ribeye five days (120 potentially billable hours) from now?

Even if you find the will to commit, the process of getting to the final product may be more exhausting than taking the California Bar Exam. After pouring over recipe books, you write out a detailed shopping list, organizing the ingredients needed by the aisles in the grocery store. When you are finished, the list takes up three full columns on legal sized paper. You encounter your first real setback, however, at the market.

You scour the aisles only to find that your market doesn't have one of the essential ingredients (usually some obscure herb, but you don't want to chance excluding it) of the twenty that you need. Since you've already wasted the better part of an hour getting all the other ingredients and you don't have your cookbook with you to change the menu, you remain driven to complete your mission. You now venture off to market #2 to find the missing item. While unpacking your bags at home, you are about to celebrate your victorious shopping excursion when you suddenly realize that you forgot that darned ribeye, the main ingredient. Exhausted and angry, you run back for a third trip where you are caught in an express line that is slower than your boss' early morning visits to the little boys' room. By the time you finally arrive home, you're annoyed and starving, causing you to binge on your EARS.

EARS is short for Emergency Atkins Recovery Supplies, *i.e.*, carb-rich foods.

Preparation of the meal is even more intimidating. What appears to be a 5-step recipe results in over an hour of labor-intensive cutting, slicing, grating, sautéing, and braising. And for all your successful multitasking at work, it all goes to hell when it comes to cooking over a hot flame—by the time you make a salad or a side dish, your main course is cold. And after three hours of cooking commitment torture, you (and possibly your company) wind up scarfing down your culinary masterpiece in three minutes. Tack on another half hour of cleaning up the dirty dishes and scrubbing the splattered kitchen and you can see why CAD #1 will make *McDonald's* a **Sister's** best friend.

CAD #2: COOKING COSTS TOO MUCH MONEY.

Yup, it's true. Buying all the ingredients you need really adds up. If you (or more likely, your husband or your mother) don't believe us, check out the following price comparison for making a Roast Chicken dinner:

Chicken:	$6.99
Spices, herbs, and condiments:	$8.25
Electric Bill for roasting:	$2.50
Your billable time to prepare chicken:	$300.00
Total cost of homemade dinner	$317.74[15]

VERSUS:

yummy Costco pre-prepared Rotisserie Roasted Chicken (that tastes better than homemade anyway) $4.99[16]

CAD #3: I DON'T HAVE THE SPACE I NEED TO PROPERLY STOCK MY KITCHEN AND COOK.

Sorry suburban **Sisters**, this whiney excuse is reserved for your city-dwelling counterparts. Take the following story from one in New York City.

Everyone wants to live in the Big Apple because they think that we all live in the Shangri-La depicted in Friends or Mad About You. But here's the real deal. Our so-called kitchen is approximately 2 x 3 feet and doubles as our foyer, which is built into the hallway connecting our entry to our all-in-one living room/family room/bedroom. Storage is so minimal that I'd rather use the scant pantry space I have to store my off-season clothes than any kitchen gadgets. Barbequing is prohibited in high-rise buildings and broiling in the oven results in setting off the fire alarm, not to mention that the nasty smell of fish or meat lingers for about a week. Because I don't drive, I can only buy items that I can carry. Oftentimes, this means I must go back and forth to the market several times like a llama just to prepare one dish. And, with a refrigerator the size of a breadbox, I have to select items by size, not by taste.

Solution? Instead of perfecting my cooking skills, I have perfected my takeout bible—it's an elaborate contracts-treatise sized binder that stores all of my delivery menus and is color-coded by cuisine and organized by number of minutes it takes the delivery guys to get to my apartment.

THE EVOLUTION OF THE SISTER COOK

As a general matter, **Sisters'** cooking habits fall into four categories, which can be viewed from an evolutionary perspective. On any given night, you could be any one of, or possess a combination of, the traits of these cooks.

The Millennium Cook

The Millennium Cook is the highest species of **Sister** cooks. You will prepare everything homemade for immediate consumption, from the bread to the pasta,[17] using only fresh and unprocessed ingredients. On the other hand, the *modified* Millennium Cook appreciates that God created fresh-frozen and prepackaged meals for a reason. This stuff can be really tasty and the presentation comparable to a four-star restaurant, although depending on the service, you may have to purchase food in quantities large enough to feed Cambodia. All you have to do is heat it up. Believe us when we tell you that you CANNOT screw it up.

The Imposter Cook

With no time to shop or cook for even a portion of the meal, what's a **Sister** to do? Well, the answer is usually, let's go out to eat. But, here is where the Millennium Cook devolves into the Imposter Cook and entertains at home on short notice. There is no reason you can't put a home-cooked meal on the table in under an hour. After all, it was home-cooked, just not in *your* home.

For example, a classic Asian-inspired Imposter Cook recipe can be mastered in three simple steps.

1) Order in two Chinese food entrees about an hour before date-time.
2) While waiting for the order, sauté some ginger in your wok (so you can smell the aroma of your fine cooking throughout your home).
3) When the order arrives, immediately place food in wok and dispose of cartons, containers, and bags in outside garbage can and squeeze contents of duck sauce, hot mustard, and soy sauce into individual little bowls.

Voilà, you've become the Iron Chef. Got a tall, dark, Mediterranean-type coming over? Follow Asian-inspired recipe above, substituting Italian for Chinese takeout, frying pan for wok, and garlic for ginger. Presto—now that's Italian!

The Martha Wanna-Be Cook

Some of us long to be Suzy-homemaker and really think that take-out or pre-prepared food is unhealthy, revolting, or just plain lame. When you feel this way but have no time on your hands to cook during the week, you may turn into the Martha wanna-be cook, whereby you do the hard work over the weekend and then enjoy the fruits of your labor all week long by freezing your work product into individual portions and heating up as needed. Of course, the downside of freezing large quantities of your favorite dish is that after a while, freezer burn will take over the taste and you will never want to eat it again (especially after your fifteenth serving).

The Cavegirl Cook (*aka* White Trash Feasting)

This is the most primitive form of cooking, usually limited to those nights you know you'll be dining in stealth-mode. Cavegirl cooks eat peanut butter (or better yet, Nutella) straight out of the jar, snack on the raw noodles in the Raman noodle mix, and polish off the whole box of *Fat-Free Snackwells* or *Lucky Charms*. The Cavegirl Cook makes eating that pint of *Ben & Jerry's* seem healthy. Don't deny it—we've all been there. Hopefully, tomorrow night you'll evolve into a more developed cooking genus, but you'll always resort back to your primal roots every once in a while.

AFTER DINNER DRINKS ANYONE?

We hope you've enjoyed our little tour through the culinary world of the Sisterhood. One conclusion can be drawn from all this food talk—there is no doubt that the practice of law is stressful. There is also no doubt that food is comforting—whether we're planning it, talking about it, cooking it, or actually eating it. So, law and food go hand in hand. As long as the food stops at the hand and doesn't turn into LASS, we concede that it's a Sisterly therapeutic favorite. Now, go drink some water.

■ ■ ■

6

For Sisters' Eyes Only

-the y-factor-

despite the increase of women in our profession, men just don't understand us. Admittedly, we can be emotional, high strung, controlling, and overly sensitive. But hell, we've got good reason—not only must we battle our raging hormones, we also must try to understand, nurture, and at times, even manipulate these guys. We now explore the unique challenges faced by Sisters, both professionally and personally, in their never-ending quest to comprehend the Y-Factor.

With two-thirds of the profession's genetic makeup containing the Y Chromosome, we can't ignore 'em, but it doesn't mean we can't try to understand 'em. There are endless differences between men and women, ranging from their inability to ask for directions to their inability to talk to the opposite sex without picturing them naked. Although you will face many Y-Factor eccentricities at some point in your practice, we focus on two of the most prevalent—the Sports Gene and the Testosterone Tyrant.

THE SPORT GENE

It's obvious—most Y-Factors are carriers of the Sports Gene, which enables them to bond with their brethren over anything sports-related. We have shoes, they have sports, what can we say? Even the most reserved Y-Factor will transform into a raving maniac as soon as another Y-Factor utters a sports score. Even if you stood in front of them butt-naked, they are too absorbed in their March Madness basketball pools or Fantasy Football drafts to care. (Okay, maybe not a good example, but you get the idea.)

Hobnobbing over the latest scores occurs in courtrooms, negotiation sessions, dog and pony shows, happy hours, parties, dinners—you name it! Our advice? If you can't beat 'em, join 'em. Knowledge is power in law—and even more so in sports. If you don't play the game (no pun intended), a Y-Factor may win over a potential client simply by engaging in a thirty-second exchange about some team's pitching staff.

Do we recommend that you memorize stats and purchase the NFL package? No, but if you can stomach it (no offense, of course, to those Sisters who actually enjoy sports), learn enough to engage in *cocktail talk*. Instead of using the sports page to line the kitty litter box, scan the headlines and topic sentences of the top stories.

Sidebar

One Sister reports that she participated in her firm's unofficial (and illegal) NCAA Basketball pool. Halfway through the tournament, the pool master distributed the stats and this Sister was leading the pack to win the $1,000 pot—100 times her initial $10 investment. When everyone got wind of her lead, she received more compliments and recognition from the male partners and senior associates—in the hallway, the cafeteria, the conference rooms, and even via email—than she EVER did for her work product. Even her boss ran into her office to ask her how she chose Marist College to beat Duke. Just think, $1000 extra bucks could almost buy you two pairs of Manolos!

But that's not all, **Sister**. We have heard from an anonymous sport-o-phile Y-Factor that modest knowledge of sports is sexier than that Victoria's Secret number that you were thinking of splurging on. So save your money for another pair of shoes and go read the sports section!

TAMING THE TESTOSTERONE TYRANT

We've all encountered the *Testosterone Tyrant* (the insidious TesTy) in our lives. The TesTy lives in all men, in varying extremes. Sometimes, it manifests itself in the member of the old boys' club who respects no one, especially women. He doesn't understand why women don't stay barefoot and pregnant. Explaining to him that you like shoes too much just doesn't fly. When he's forced to work with you, he will either withhold all challenging assignments or will crush you with them, mostly because he thinks you can't handle *man's work* or you will eventually crash and burn into the maternal wall.

Trying to convince him that you're just as capable as your Brother-in-Law counterparts is like trying to talk a meter maid out of a parking ticket. The best you can do is to know the law and your case or the deal as well as you know the aisles at Ferragamo. The only way to win an inkling of respect from this beast is to show him how smart you are and how willing you are to work hard for him.

The TesTy also shows up in the slimy, slithery guy who is incapable of looking at women without seeing breasts or asses. His crass comments about **Sisters'** body parts and sexual fantasies make even the most tolerant Brothers-in-Law cringe. Luckily, we girls made a great friend in 1964 named *Title VII* who can be one mean bitch when it comes to being sexually harassed at the workplace. Appropriate conduct is now beaten into the heads (no pun intended) of all male associates as soon as they enter the office, but that doesn't mean that all will be cleansed completely of their Neanderthal habits. Although the law does not protect an occasional, offensive remark, if the behavior or remarks create what you believe to be a hostile environment, report it right away. Chances are, this bad apple has been rotting away at the office for too long and it's time for your employer to clean house.

THE MAGNETIC FORCE BETWEEN THE Y-CHROMOSOME AND THE X-CHROMOSOME

Enough about dealing with the Y-Factor on a professional level— let's focus on the fun stuff now. Namely, how do you find your soulmate while practicing law? Before we try to explore the murky world of the dating patterns of the Y-Factor, we need to step back and do a little psychoanalysis on ourselves.

Sisters' Most Common Personality Disorders

By now, you must have realized that there are certain characteristics and communication styles women have to which men will never relate. Many of these traits cultivate into full-blown personality disorders when you become a member of the Sisterhood. Let us share with you a few of the most common disorders (and we use this word only in the most endearing way).

ANAL-RETENTIVE DISORDER

Within weeks of beginning law practice, we become obsessed with punctuation, grammar, spelling, and even word spacing. Closely related is our compulsion to tab, file, color code, and numerically stamp anything that lands on our desk, including the Chinese takeout menu. All of this accumulates into a full-blown case of Anal-Retentive Disorder.

MULTITASKING MADNESS DISORDER

With an overwhelming number of personal and professional demands on us each and every day, we use the Multitasking Madness Disorder in search of balance. Out of necessity you become a pro at researching and writing memos, surfing for potential lunch venues on Zagat.com, cutting the split ends off of your hair, reapplying lipstick, emailing your buddies, and doing Kegels,[18] all while participating in a three-way conference call.

CAUSE AND EFFECT DISORDER

Soon after you begin studying for the LSAT, the Cause and Effect Disorder starts. The art of logic is beaten into your head with crazy hypotheticals involving ten people at a table. When all ten people move spots 10,000 times and you are asked to identify where little Joey winds up, you can't help but scratch your head and wonder, *who cares*? However, since this test can make or break your chances of getting into a good law school, you not only care about the result, you become obsessed with knowing why Joey would move spots 10,000 times. No longer are you satisfied with the answer, *shit happens*. Everything has to happen for a distinct reason that must be supported by clear and convincing evidence.

PERFECTION DISORDER

All it takes is getting reamed by your client or boss on a wholly insignificant mistake and WHAM, you are afflicted with Perfection Disorder and vow to be 200% perfect forever.

DELEGATION DEFICIT DISORDER (AKA MICROMANAGING)

When a paralegal, secretary, or junior associate you delegated work to makes a small blunder, the Delegation Deficit Disorder attacks and never again will you confidently delegate anything to anyone without worrying and obsessing that they screwed up. In fact, you won't want to delegate anything because it will lead to your spending seven times as long checking and correcting it.

TIME IS MONEY DISORDER

For those of you who unfortunately are judged by the quantity, not quality, of the hours that you bill, every nonbillable minute must be time well spent. In these situations the Time is Money Disorder sets in.

POST-CLOSE/POST-FILING EUPHORIA DISORDER

After slaving around the clock for days or even weeks at a time, this Post-Close/Post-Filing Euphoria Disorder kicks in the second a big deal closes or a big motion is filed with the court. This overwhelming feeling of happiness and invincibility is immediately followed by a complete shutdown—total uselessness and laziness.

THE GROSS RATIONALIZATION DISORDER

The Gross Rationalization Disorder enables us to rationalize anything we do, no matter how imprudent or stupid, because we have very little time to ourselves. It usually manifests itself in retail therapy.

— Sidebar —

The Dating Dilemma for Sisters

Let's see how these disorders play out in the dating world.

You have a blind date scheduled for the Saturday night after one of your big deals finally closes. Mr. Blind Date calls to schedule a pick up time, but naturally, you have *Post-Close Euphoria* Disorder and you are so tired it's difficult to act enthusiastic. You didn't catch up on your sleep last night because you wound up reorganizing your shoe collection until 3 a.m. when you were in the midst of searching for your date-shoes (*Anal-Retentive Disorder*), so you are less than excited to hear from him. You then decide that none of the 200 pairs of shoes in your closet are good date shoes, so you run out to the mall where you drop $450 on the latest

Guccis. But that's okay because you never have time to shop and you're much too busy to wait for a sale. (*Gross Rationalization Disorder.*)

Your date is approximately six minutes late picking you up because the President is in town and all highways are closed. The nerve of him (your blind date, not the President). This just cost you $50 in bill-ables—that's your *Time is Money Disorder* kicking in—so now you are annoyed. You notice that he has a pretty bad five-o'clock shadow going on and you have the almost uncontrollable urge to pumice your feet (something you forgot to do in the shower that day) on his face. The *Perfection Disorder* leaves you anxious and distracted.

Despite starting off on the wrong foot, you have a really nice din-ner. Due to his unforgivable act of booking a first-date dinner at a non-Zagat's Top 50 pick (where you are accustomed to dining a la firm or client), you take it upon yourself to plan—in nitty-gritty detail—all of your future dates with him (your *Delegation Deficit Disorder* rearing its ugly head). Because of your work schedule, future dates become a lot of time on the phone with him, while you simultaneously write a brief, do your nails, walk your dog, or wash your hair (what did we do before the speakerphone?). This will annoy him because you will never really be listening to what he's saying (a cruel byproduct of your *Multitasking Madness Disorder*).

After a few months of seeing each other, you have now cancelled about 90% of your dates because of work-related emergencies. He lets you know that he's not interested in dating you anymore. Instead of getting upset, you demand to know the particulars of what you did to cause this unexpected breakup. And there Sister, is your *Cause and Effect Disorder* at its finest.

The Dating Dilemma

Now **Sisters**, we know you are perfect in every way, and it's hard to believe you don't have suitors knocking down your door, but we just wanted to point out that dating may be a tad bit harder than if you were a humble non-**Sister**. The longer you practice, the more particular and demanding you become because you are programmed for perfection in your work. You expect no less in your personal life. The most trivial flaw or annoyance becomes a deal breaker. Thus, all **Sisters** sooner or later experience the Dating Dilemma.

Nevertheless, we will continue the arduous search for Mr. Right. During this search, you will be faced with some dating decisions your mother never warned you about.

Maximizing Your Second Shift

How do you master the sport of dating when you're never home before 9 p.m. most nights? Find yourself another nocturnal worker and make the most of the second shift. We note that if you start a date after 11 p.m., as many **Sisters** report they do, there is a high probability that the date will end in one of two ways:

(1) if your date is a total dud, you will turn into a pumpkin by midnight or

(2) if you are really lonely or horny, your date will continue until the next morning. In other words, sleepovers are almost a given for any guy who doesn't put you to sleep after the first five minutes.

Even if you feel so-so about the Y-Factor candidate, in the back of your demented little mind, you know that sex has far fewer calories than that large pizza you will polish off if you send Mr. So-So on his merry way. And since you didn't go to the gym that day, you might as well burn some calories doing the nasty, even if you stare at the bedroom ceiling the entire time counting the minutes (in six minute increments, of course) until it is over (Time is Money Disorder).

Let us not forget another benefit of dating during the second shift—the added bonus of car service or dinners a la client, which will make you look like a big shot.

If your date meets you at the office, we Sisters are all in agreement that even the most innocent sexual encounters anywhere in the firm are strictly TABOO. With all the nocturnal creatures running around at the office, the walls will talk—trust us!

SISTERS DATING BROTHERS—INCESTUOUS?

What happens when you lock up hormonally charged lawyers in their 20's and 30's in a building for days at a time barring any contact with the outside world? You guessed it, Sister—sex, sex, and more sex. When we enter this noble profession, many of us take a vow never to date at the office. It will be easy at first because you will think all of your colleagues are boring, annoying, and repulsive. After you live at the office for a few weeks and lose contact with your non-Sister friends, however, your colleagues who are still boring and annoying are now desirable and worthy. Take it from us, incestuous dating (Sisters dating Brothers-in-Law) is as common as developing blisters after wearing a brand new pair of pumps.

Although interoffice dating can't do anything good for your reputation at the office, we must admit that having a little fling may make an otherwise unbearable place just a tad more interesting. It will also provide you with some much needed TLC and an ally only a few floors away when you have been tormented day after day by a TesTy or BBQ.

Most inter-firm affairs follow a certain paradigm that goes something like this. The dating (or *flinging* in the case of commitment-phobe **Sisters**) will start after glaring into each others' beer goggle eyes after some late night holiday party or closing dinner. Afraid that her fragile little reputation will be tarnished (even if nobody knows who she is), she will behave as clandestine as a politician having an affair with an intern.

On more than one occasion, we have witnessed a **Sister** and her flame snuggling up on the subway ride into the office, sharing a latte and musing over the previous night's sleepover party. As soon as the **Sister** gets out of the station, she and Mr. Associate *du jour* part like the Red Sea, not even so much as looking at each other in the elevator bank.

Funny thing is, this so-called secret is known already by EVERYONE, because law firms (even more so than law schools) are like high school and gossip spreads like wildfire. This is attributable mostly to the fact that people at the office are so bored with their own lives. The grand irony of the paradigm, of course, is that once the **Sister** and Brother go public, it will be interesting for about seven hours (the average amount of time a nonlawyer spends at the firm per day) and then you're old news.

This affair will end in one of two ways. Either the couple will fall blissfully in love and marry, or they will have a nasty breakup that everyone will know the details of, and one of them will leave the firm.

There is one exception to this paradigm—the AA (not alcoholic's anonymous, but the Adulterous Affair). In this scenario, a middle-aged married partner, a geekoid his whole life, who was not blessed with good looks and married Wife #1 while in law school, starts earning big bucks and suddenly turns into a babe magnet. When he secretly starts dating young pretty associate, everyone knows about it but no one talks about it because they are afraid of being sacked by power partner. When Shuga Daddy divorces Wife #1 to marry Wife #2 (young pretty associate), the new wife instantly gives up law practice to become a private investigator. Paranoid that her adulterous husband will trade her in for a new flavor of the month, she keeps close tabs on his every move.

Just remember, as tempting as this situation may or may not sound, what goes around comes around!

Sisters Dating Nonlawyers—Kosher?

The demarcation between lawyers and nonlawyers in a law office is like night and day. However, the computer guy who recovers your forty page Summary Judgment Motion at 2 a.m. will appear irresistible and the delivery guy who gets it to the courthouse by 4:59 p.m. will appear, well, just plain hot. Be forewarned of one thing (we apologize for sounding condescending here even though we are), to the copy and filing guys, you are their Shuga Mama—their ticket to the other side of the tracks.

— Sidebar —

In our experience, the yummiest guys in the office are typically the transitional paralegals, many of whom are right out of college, still fresh, buff (note the distinct lack of LASS), and untainted by long hours working in fluorescent lighting. Many Sister associate/male paralegal relationships blossom at large firms, particularly where the paralegal needs a good recommendation for law school. Our advice? Resist the temptation or wait until one of you has left the firm.

MARITAL MAYHEM

So, you finally found Mr. Right who loves you despite all your lawyer-like eccentricities and crazy relatives. And, did we forget to mention that yes, he proposed to you bearing a boulder the size of Gilbraltar that you most definitely deserve. Now you will need to conquer a task even more daunting than going to trial or running a billion dollar deal—planning the big day while still practicing law. **Sisters**, if we spent as much time negotiating the fine print of our prenuptial agreement as we devote to the details of our over-the-top after-party and honeymoon, divorces would be far less messy.

Surviving Your Engagement

Because we perfected the Multitasking Madness Disorder, we think that we can do it all ourselves. Also contributing to this primal urge is our Delegation Deficit Disorder—no matter what anyone does to help you with the planning, it won't be as good as if you do it yourself. There's also no price we won't pay for the best. Even if we can get it cheaper, the opportunity cost (time away from work and cost of foregoing billable hours) of finding a better deal exceeds the savings (Gross Rationalization Disorder). We don't even need to tell you how the Anal-Retentive Disorder rears its ugly little head in the process of wedding planning.

In our experience, as well as the experience of every **Sister** we know, Mr. Future-Husband's only contribution to planning the big day and honeymoon will be showing up (and he will probably be late unless his mother nudges him to death).

There are a few ways in which being a **Sister** provides you with fantastic skills in the wedding planning area. First, due to your Perfection Disorder and Delegation Deficiency Disorder, you will trust no one to follow through on anything, so you can be sure that no stone will go unturned. Second, whether you are a litigator or a transactional negotiator, you will have no qualms about haggling down the price on everything. Most of the prices quoted by your vendors have a lot of room for negotiation, so don't be shy about testing the savings waters (with the exception, of course, of trying to negotiate the fees charged by your clergymen. Haggling with God can only get you into trouble).

If you don't elope to Vegas, you are also faced with the painful decision of whom you will invite from your office. At a large firm you are not expected to invite everyone, so apply the general rule of law (ah, can't get away from that lawyerese). Invite your Bingin' and Bitchin' Buddies and Saintly Mentors. Don't even think about excluding your secretary, *aka* party planning assistant. And don't waste your time inviting lawyers you want to suck up to. Let's face it, the Muckety-Mucks have better things to do with their nonexistent free time than eat piggies-in-a-blanket and cough up enough money to cover their seats at the wedding of a suck-up they couldn't pick out of a police lineup. Oh, and don't forget, even if you love to complain to your family and friends about how much you hate a particular partner, make sure you brainwash them not to repeat anything negative at the wedding festivities, especially after one too many Cosmopolitans.

To Change or Not Change Your Maiden Name

TheKnot.com reports that over *eighty* percent of women today change their maiden names.[19] We find this study statistically flawed based on our own observations. Generally speaking, our midwestern and southern Sisters tend to support changing their last name while those on the West Coast generally favor using their maiden name professionally and their husband's name socially. Ball-busting New York Sisters snub their nose at giving up their maiden name for any man.

Changing your name can make your life easier if you have children, monogrammed towels, or your maiden name rhymes with a female body part. Making reservations is a simpler task, although there's something perversely sexy about checking into a hotel under two different last names. And let us not forget, changing your name means you can hide from solicitors and ghosts of your dating past.

While you will earn brownie points with your mother-in-law for carrying on the torch, understand that at some point in your life, you will be called *Mrs. So and So*—are you prepared for that? Also consider whether your husband's ego is tough enough to withstand the telemarketing calls looking for Mr. **Sister's** Last Name. And most importantly, you will be able to play the *I gave up my parents' name for you* trump card again and again and again during any marital quarrels.

Sisters who were admitted to practice law before they got married will enjoy even more hassles than the rest of the population when they change their last names. When you are a lawyer, entering the witness protection program may seem an easier task than taking on your spouse's last name. Because you are granted a license by the state in which you took the bar, you are not entitled to practice law under any name other than the one printed on your pretty admittance certificate. Therefore, you will have to change your name with all the courts, bars (state bars, that is), and every one else who has any record of your existence practicing law. In many jurisdictions, this is a big fat pain-in-the-LASS.

Two highly rated name-change kits are *The Official New Bride Name Change Kit*, **www.kitbiz.com** and *Wedding Sense Name Change Guide and Kit for New Brides*, **www.bridekit.com**.

Wearing the Cute Pants in the Family

Despite your parents' advice to *marry money, you'll learn to love him*, you may not have married your Shuga Daddy. In households with two working spouses, 33% of the wives earned more money than their husbands.[20] We suspect that percentage is closer to 50% where the wife is a **Sister**, as law is among the top paying professions in our country (despite the fact that after fat, lack of money is the second most prevalent complaint out of any **Sister's** mouth). In other words, your chances of scoring a Shuga Daddy are just about equal to your chances of becoming a Shuga Mama.

When you do marry for love (and hopefully good sex to boot) and not money, there are a few potential pitfalls of which you should be aware. If you are both working, you will continue to be stuck with most household duties and responsibilities—unless you put an end to the madness. No matter how *Leave It to Beaver* your husband wants his life to be, the fact of the matter is that you're bringing in as much, if not more money to your household, and that means everyone should have his or her share of laundry, cleaning, cooking, and other errand responsibilities. If your husband finds these tasks emasculating, tell him that you will hire a live-in maid to do the *woman's work* with the money he would have spent on season tickets to some important men-in-spandex games, or worse yet, his country club membership.

The upside of wearing the cute pants? Although you won't have the unlimited budget you believe you are entitled to and you won't be able to take an indefinite maternity leave, wearing the cute pants in the family is not without rewards. First, you will have the ability to buy anything you want for yourself and indulge in *juicy lunches* without asking his permission. Second, Tarzan will no longer rule the coop. If you are bringing home the low-fat, low-sodium turkey bacon, you get an equal or greater vote on how to fry it up in a pan. This frying power extends to investments, remote control time, social plans, offsprings' names, infant care, and last but not least, workout priority.

Juicy lunches— buying skinny designer jeans during lunch instead of consuming highly caloric food.

■ ■ ■

So now you're hitched. Join us for some more adventures through the next chapter of your life as a **Sister**—one that is likely to be filled with heartburn, nausea, incontinence, and ultimately, sleep-deprivation. Got any clues?

7

Out of the Frying Pan, Into the Fire

-sisterhood meets motherhood-

beep! Beep! Beep! No, it's not your heart rate or your annoying alarm clock blasting you out of a deep sleep. It's your biological clock going off. But where did the time go? Assuming you didn't take time off to *find yourself* after high school or college, you won't graduate law school until you are about 25 years old. For at least the next five years, you sell your soul to the work devil, dedicating every waking moment to learning the ropes. Due to your rigorous schedule and high-standards, you probably don't find Mr. Right until you are in your late 20's or early 30's.

Once hitched, you may consider postponing the trying to conceive (TTC) phase until well into your mid to late thirties, at which time biology is sadly not always a **Sister's** best friend. We wish we could tack an extra ten years onto our clocks, a so-called *working and marrying decade.* Even though we are a powerful voice, sorrowfully we have yet to strike a deal with God to attain a biological clock extension. So, as luck would have it, our prime billing years overlap with our prime reproductive years. If Carrie Bradshaw from *Sex in The City* were a **Sister**, this episode would begin with the burning question—*Is it possible for* **Sisters** *to synchronize their biological clocks with their billing clocks?*

TAKING THE PREGNANCY PLUNGE

Despite our obsessive-compulsive, risk-averse nature, when it comes to having children, all our neuroses seem to fly out the window. Weirdly enough, while we plan everything in our lives down to whether or not we will be having an omelet with or without yolks a week from next Tuesday, many of us admit to TTC the second after:

- we learn our last **Sister** friend got knocked up or
- we read the media's exploitation of the latest declining fertility study in women of *mature ages.*[21]

Some **Sisters** even admit to taking the pregnancy plunge as a knee-jerk reaction to job dissatisfaction, despite the fact that they were historically repulsed by the mere presence of young children, baby talk, and poopy diapers. For the rest of us, the decision to conceive may happen something like this.

After putting in a full ten-hour day at the office, you are exhausted. You stumble home, and finally fall into a coma-like state on the couch, where the only thing you can do is curl into your darling hubby's arms and stare at pictures in In-Style Magazine *(and wish you actually had time to buy ANYTHING). All of a sudden, your husband takes your hand, gives you a kiss and says, "Honey, you are the kindest, smartest, most beautiful woman in the world, and there's nothing I want more than a child who is exactly like you." And with that, you're off to the marital sack sans birth control. And in two weeks, perhaps for the first time in your life, you won't be making deals with God if only you would get your period.*

Of course, if you suffer (even a tad) from *Anal-Retentive Disorder,* before tossing out your birth control, you may wish to research your employer's pregnancy leave policies and state and federal pregnancy leave laws. If your office does not have a formal maternity leave policy, find out if there is an unwritten policy (*i.e.*, if other **Sisters** blazed the trail before you). Lastly, find out what kind of benefits, if any, you will receive if you are forced to go on bed rest and watch *Oprah* all day long.

If you are not already covered by your employer, consider purchasing an individual disability policy for extra protection. Don't forget to check out the Family and Medical Leave Act and call the Family and Job-Survival Hotline at 800-522-0925 (run by National Association of Working Women). It provides information on family leave laws in your state.

VOLUNTARY DISCLOSURE? MAKING THE BIG ANNOUNCEMENT

Congratulations! After all your worrying about the family jewels, turns out his boys can swim. Now you are faced with the inevitable question—*When do I spill the beans?*

Survey says—twelve weeks, which is after your first trimester, because the risk of miscarriage exponentially decreases.

But who are we kidding? You will probably tell your Bingin' and Bitchin' Buddies about thirty seconds after you see that telltale pink line on the pregnancy test—which is about fifteen minutes before you tell the father of your child.

Of course, there is a more superficial, but nonetheless compelling, rea-

The twelve-week rule has its exceptions. If you excuse yourself to go to the little girl's room seventeen times during a deposition, you may have to tell sooner. Unfortunately, you will have no choice but to tell the second after you puke on your boss's $30,000 desk during a conference call.

son that will give you a burning desire to drop the bomb before the twelve-week mark—at some point in your first trimester, you will start to look, well, not pregnant, but just plain thick. Sort of like how you would look if you dined at *KFC* and *Dairy Queen* for three meals a day, seven days a week. Since we all suffer from the Perfection Disorder, the thought of anyone thinking that you are even a little chubbier than last week will just about kill you. If we can give you any advice after bearing our own kiddies, however, it is this—the longer you can wait to tell the chieftains, the better. This is particularly true if you are a Bubble Associate (although we're not sure how you would have found the time to conceive in this case) or if it's right before bonus season.

Now, you obviously don't want to wait until you've broken your water on your partner's Gucci loafers, but if you can prove that you can incubate another human being as well as doing as much work as is necessary in order to get by, let them think you're porking out for as long as possible.

How will the news be received? Some report that their pregnancy experience at work was akin to that "of a leper at a public square."[22] Others felt that their employers were outwardly excited, but behind closed doors, their long-term commitment to their job was questioned. Without exception, however, you will find that any other prego or recently prego **Sister** will instantly become your best friend, even if she had been a total—dare we say it—bitch to you before. All of a sudden, all the formerly standoffish, arrogant **Sisters** in the office want to see pictures from your ultrasound and share labor and delivery horror stories with you, so take advantage of their gentility while you can.

THE FINE ART OF PRACTICING PREGO

Anyone who's been there will tell you that being prego is an *entire* out-of-body experience. The person you formerly remember as you becomes possessed by raging hormones and a Rubenesque woman carrying an extra thirty to sixty pounds stares back at you in the mirror. This other human being growing inside of you (defined herein as the Possession) turns you into one Possessed Sister. We want to share with you some of the unique experiences you may encounter as a Possessed Sister while practicing law and how to deal with them (or not deal, but at the very least, laugh about them).

Rubenesque—
this is a favorite term used by Internet dating services to categorize *fat* as something mildly sexy. (We have been told by Brothers that no one is really fooled by this description.)

The Weight Gain

We don't think any Sister has ever gotten pregnant without some sort of nagging anxiety about gaining and losing all the baby weight. And be prepared—not all of it is in your tummy. You may feel you are carrying another child in your ass, arms, thighs, and even breasts, because these body parts oftentimes grow in proportion to your tummy.

—— Sidebar ——

It should be noted that your breasts grow before everything else catches up, so for a while you will look like a porn star. And no, your husband will not reap the benefits of these new toys, because you'll feel too green, too tired, and/or too worried that you will damage the growing embryo, to have sex.

Although you want to maintain your professional image, this is no time to rush out and spend big bucks on maternity clothes. Even the most expensive threads are typically made of some synthetic polyester fibers (because they stretch) that will not only make you look large, but will also make you sweat. What we're saying here is save your money for your post-baby skinny clothes. To the extent you can, beg, borrow, and steal from other recently Possessed **Sisters** in your office or from other friends who are willing to share. And don't worry—no one is going to be doing a fashion check on a Possessed **Sister**, so you have our permission to wear the same black pants and boring white blouse almost everyday.

As you get bigger and bigger, you will no longer see your feet, which is a good thing because they typically turn into large sausage-links. As much as we hate to advise it, you will need to invest in a good pair of sturdy, ugly, wide shoes at the end, because you won't even be able to get your big toe into your strappy Manolos.

> Don't let your ugly shoes morph into the shoe-clump mountain, because you will not be able to bend over to sort them out.

Although you will feel like a beached whale for a good part of your pregnancy, for the first time in your life, you will be given a reprieve from the Perfection Disorder when it comes to fat and your body. Of course, you will probably shift all this negative energy into obsessing over the health of your child or those nasty pre-school applications, but at least you won't be quite as interested in your husband's insipid response to the *Does this make my ass look fat* question (which he never answers correctly anyway).

Peeing and Puking

Possessed **Sisters** will probably spend more time in the bathroom than at their desks. Since you can't move your desk into the bathroom, drain frequently, especially before those three-hour depositions or conference calls commence. Towards the end of the pregnancy, however, you may notice that your timing is off, particularly when you cough, sneeze, or laugh a bit too hard. Although you will think everyone else in the room must know that you should be wearing Depends, they will have no idea, particularly if you're wearing that black pair of pants discussed earlier.

No sooner will you get used to the incessant urge to pee than you will start to feel a little queasy (typically between your 8ᵗʰ and 12ᵗʰ week). This can range from a mild nausea (*i.e.*, like you ate too much cookie batter) to full blown head-in-the-toilet, nonstop retching all day long.

Some authors of pregnancy books and other people who profess to be pregnancy experts claim that morning sickness is some psychological manifestation of your reluctance to be a mother. You have our personal permission to flog such people (although if called to testify on your behalf, we will categorically deny ever giving you this permission).

Morning sickness (truly a misnomer, because it can strike you at any time of the day) is as real as that rock on your finger had better be. As counterintuitive as it sounds, the best way to combat booting is to keep eating. Of course, binging will send you right back to the porcelain goddess, but bite-size snacking may do the trick.

Unfortunately, when you're at the height of this sickness, nothing anyone can say or do will make you feel better. Even the old tickle of the tonsils doesn't provide relief. The best we can tell you is that it does eventually pass and if you tell your office you need to take some time off due to the stomach flu or food poisoning, it is a far from unprecedented little fib.

The Great Brain Drain

While you are Possessed, your body is a chemistry lab and the hormone cocktails mulling about in your blood are enough to make you go crazy. Most notably, you will experience *Brain Drain*. Some of the classic symptoms are strangely found in many a fairy tale character.

SLEEPING BEAUTY

During the first trimester, many **Sisters** experience a lovely glow as well as stronger and healthier hair and nails than they ever had before (probably attributable to the vitamins they now don't forget to take). Problem is, you are too darn tired to take advantage of this new-found beauty. You swear you could sleep forever and probably will sleep through most of your meetings and conference calls. Although you will regain some consciousness during your second trimester, by the end of your third trimester your brain will be in a vegetative state. And when you take away Sleeping Beauty's diet staples—coffee and Diet Coke—she is not only more fatigued, but she can be one mean bitch.

HUMPTY DUMPTY

The symptom categorized as Humpty Dumpty is so dubbed not because you are big and round (which you are), but because your emotions are always teetering on the wall, ready to shatter at any second of the day. When your secretary hands you an unsolicited blackline along with the clean draft of the latest deal document, you hug her and tell her how much you love her. Conversely, when your husband picks up 1% milk instead of skim, you go apoplectic. You will need to get used to this extreme sensitivity and try to not fall off your wall, despite the fact that you are one step away from spontaneously combusting.

GRETEL (AS IN HANSEL AND...)

Remember how Gretel got lost in the woods and forgot her way home? You too, will start to forget some pretty basic things as the millions of cells multiplying to create a human being in your belly are borrowing from the cell storage in your brain. You must leave your crumbs (i.e., extensive to-do lists), just like Gretel and her brother did, if you are ever going to find your way home at the end of a day.

The good news is most people (particularly the Ancient Relics whose wives were actually barefoot and pregnant) will be very understanding and sympathetic. For the rest of the lot, the Preggers Trump Card will save your scatterbrained, Possessed butt most of the time.

Playing the Preggers Trump Card

The *Preggers Trump Card* (PTC) is your get out of jail free card. Need a continuance, extension, or late trial date? Invoke the PTC. Don't want to get put on a deal or an assignment that will extend through your due date? Call in the PTC, which incidentally becomes even more effective if you mention certain buzz words, such as *contractions* or *high risk pregnancy*.

The PTC is also a tactical defense for sleeping at your desk, forgetting insignificant assignments, and basically not living up to your normal 200% perfect work product.

We should note that much of the time, you won't even have to invoke the PTC to enjoy the fruits of the card. You see, the Y-Factor is typically deathly afraid of anything that has to do with *feminine issues*, including, of course, anything having to do with your Possessed state. For better or worse, most Y-Factors will probably take it easy on you.

If you happen to run late, forget an assignment, or just plain space out during a conference call, simply explain to your Y-Factor boss that you're feeling some lower groin pain because your uterus is compressed by the amniotic sac and your elevated progesterone levels. Watch your boss turn eight shades of red, stare at his shoes, and blurt out *no problem* as he starts sweating profusely.

But remember, the PTC is an omnipotent little gift that expires along with your Possessed state, so use it wisely. For example, if one of your Bingin' and Bitchin' Buddies gets stuck with your PTC dump, you will pay if and when you return from *Maternity Vacation*.

Responding to Discovery Requests about your Future and Planning for your Vacation

While you are Possessed, your bosses may try to serve interrogatories on you with respect to your long-term plans.

No matter what your plans are, invoke the LIE technique and repeat after us, *of course I will return full-time*. Not only will it preserve your current situation and paid maternity leave, but it will also increase your bargaining position when they expect you back and you are on the fence.

Many **Sisters** try to work until their contractions are about seven minutes apart in order to prove what troopers they are. But the real reason we do it is to save all of our maternity leave time until after Junior arrives so that we can maximize time at the gym shedding Junior-fat and enjoying time with Junior (not necessarily in that order). At many firms, **Sisters** are forced to begin leave about two weeks before their due date. At the less formal firms, it starts when someone spots you carrying a towel around in case your water breaks. Either way, during your final days you should make sure to wind down and meet with your boss to make a plan for how your work will be covered while you are out. Whatever you do, prepare a written memo detailing the status of each client matter in the hopes of preventing the work-related phone call that will inevitably occur in the middle of a lactation consultant's visit.

So now you're ready to become a Mommy. Come and join us on your Maternity Vacation and what follows.

Interrogatories are a set of questions one party sends to the opposing party in litigation requesting them to provide information relevant to the lawsuit signed under penalty of perjury.

MOTHERHOOD, NOW WHAT?

Congratulations! You've survived your hospital stay. Forgive us for not warning you about what the birthing process was really like. If we had done so, you probably would have sued God for an injunction because childbirth certainly qualifies as cruel and unusual punishment. But now you've been there, done that, and you're thinking, let's get this three-month holiday on the road, right? Time to shop at Sak's, go for a daily run, and do lunch with the ladies, all while Junior snoozes away in his Frog.

Remember when you used to scoff at all those pathetic non-Sister mommies who complained about lack of sleep and the horrid first few months of childrearing. As a Sister, you thought, *Hey, I have pulled all-nighters in law school and at the firm on a regular basis, solved Einstein-like logic questions on the bar exam in under two minutes, and wrestled with the biggest sharks in town over billion dollar matters. C'mon, how difficult could it be when my only responsibility is a little 10-pound mass that sleeps most of the time?* Think again. Ask anyone who has given birth (other than those who employ a full-time staff to take care of Junior and all other household obligations) about the first six weeks of her maternity leave and you will understand that it truly is the vacation gone bad.

Because you cannot shop for designer skinny clothes for a few weeks (or months!) after giving birth, you may wish to keep up with the latest Mommy Fashions with the ultimate prego status symbol *du jour*: your buggy. At the time of this print, the Bugaboo Frog was the see and be seen overpriced status stroller.

Maternity Leave—The Vacation Gone Bad

You arrive home with your little one ready to begin perfecting your new 18-year work product. Perhaps for the first few days, your mini-**Sister** sleeps through the night, and again you mock whiney non-**Sister** mommies. Then week two sets in. Nothing you can do stops the 24-hour crying. Being the oh so power **Sister** that you are, however, you know you can handle the all-nighters, despite the fact that you have not hired or asked for help (remember, you suffer from Delegation Deficiency Disorder so you think you can do it all, and better, by yourself).

By week four, you have not slept in 21 days. Even when you lived at the printer's for a month, you still got to catch a good night's sleep every few days. You can't remember how to spell your child's name; you have no idea what day of the week it is; you haven't showered in three days; and, to top it off, the style *du jour* in your house is now a nursing bra and pajama bottoms.

So where is darling da-da when you are on your last legs fighting the nocturnal 10-pound demon? It is our duty to inform you about a scant talked-about, but serious condition that affects almost all new fathers: the Hearing Impaired New Dad Syndrome (the HINDS). You will know that your husband has contracted this ghastly ailment when he becomes legally deaf between the hours of 10 p.m. and 7 a.m., and awakes each morning with bruised shins from a **Sister's** ineffectual attempt to kick his butt out of bed.

As sleep-deprived as you feel, your Multitasking Madness Disorder will lead you to believe that since you are not working, you should be able to maintain a tidy house, cook dinner, go shopping, read your emails, and even call into work on a daily basis. Unfortunately, however, for the first time in your life, multitasking is a near impossibility (despite reports from most **Sisters** that they can accomplish a few of the above tasks while simultaneously nursing).

By week six, when you look around at your helter-skelter home, your nocturnal baby, and your HINDS patient, you will enter the panic-zone, which is only aggravated by your Anal-Retentive

Disorder and Perfection Syndrome. It is about this point that many **Sisters** realize that *this vacation sucks* and begin to get jealous of their husbands when they leave for work.

If you think that you can do some work from home while on maternity leave, think again. While most employers seem to respect a **Sister's** maternity leave time, there are some who will not. It all starts with, what seems like innocuous telephone calls. Then, you visit the office to show off your little queen. The next thing you know, the secretaries grab your princess out of your arms, leaving you sitting in an ongoing conference call. Before you know it, your lunch with the boss ends at 6 p.m. with your filling out your time-sheets at your desk and your sleeping baby waking up in a fit of rage.

While the money and intellectual stimulation may look attractive during these early weeks, listen to us when we tell you—your child will only be this young ONCE, so don't get sucked back in too fast. Remember, you really need some time to get used to your new boarder before you add the stress of your everyday **Sisterly** demands.

Plus, over the next few weeks, it gets easier and even, dare we say it, fun. And, just when you get the whole baby thing figured out and you can squeeze into some of your skinny clothes again, your maternity leave is over. For this reason alone, we suspect that the drafters of the Family Medial Leave Act must have included at least one TesTy.

Putting Motherhood above Sisterhood

If you have married your Shuga Daddy or you are otherwise financially able to take a break from practicing so that you can devote your full-time attention to your little angel(s), you will be faced with the choice of whether to put Motherhood above **Sisterhood**. This decision is not always an easy one and you will probably mull it over with many of your friends before you make your ultimate decision (although we must warn you that you risk serious bodily harm to you or your baby if you complain about your dilemma to **Sisters** who have not been provided with such a financial choice).

Many actually scoff at the notion of hitting the glass ceiling, because really, they opt out of the rat race before even getting to that point. For those **Sisters** on the partnership track, however, the choice is difficult. While you will have an unlimited budget to purchase designer shoes or anything else you desire, your workload and rainmaking responsibilities will quadruple, resulting in even less time than you already have—which wasn't nearly enough before you had Junior.

We are here to tell you that if you can afford it and you feel it is your calling to be a stay-at-home mommy (SAHM)—BY ALL MEANS DO SO AND DO NOT FEEL GUILTY! YOUR CAREER IS NOT OVER BY A LONG SHOT!

You see, unlike almost any other profession, we are blessed with permanent skills that transcend time. Your degree and experience are probably the best insurance policies you can buy. Even if you don't want to go back to practicing law, the skills you have acquired enable you to do a myriad of things, not the least of which is win many a PTA argument.

If you do choose the sacred life of the SAHM, resist the uncontrollable urge to treat your new bundle of joy as an associate in training. Try to keep in mind (we know, easier said than done) that although you can't spell-check, shepardize, and grammar-proof your child, he or she will always be your finest accomplishment in life, even if he or she doesn't get into the Harvard nursery school feeder *du jour*.

One last thing that is worth mentioning here. When we first set out to write this book, one of the main themes we wanted to address was *Is it possible to have it all? Can you really be a super-power partner and super-mommie at the same time?* Sadly, not one **Sister** we interviewed responded an emphatic *yes* to this question. For those of you who become SAHMs with the intention of returning to the workforce at some point in the future, we are hopeful that someday you will be able to say *you can have it all, but just not at the same time.*

RETURNING TO THE ~~FIRE~~ FIRM

If you ask Mommy-**Sisters** why they returned to work after their maternity leave expired, about 95% of them will give you a one-word response—money. Sadly, personal satisfaction in practicing law rarely topped any new mommy's list. If you are going back purely for the money, rest assured, leaving your precious baby in the arms of another, whether it is your mom, your stay-at-home husband, or someone you pay, will be the hardest thing you ever do. You will fantasize about moving to a shack in the middle of a third world country where money isn't needed just so you can stay in your hut and never leave Junior's side.

If you are feeling this way, trust us when we tell you that the anticipation of going back to work is probably the most horrible part, followed by the first week back.

> Start your first week back on a Thursday or Friday, because five days back in the office will throw you into **Sisterly**-shock after a three-month maternity stint.

Most **Sisters** report that things fall into place and they develop a routine that they, their HINDS patients, and their babies are comfortable with. After all, consider the advantages of returning to the war zone. If you're not swamped, you get out for uninterrupted mani's/pedi's, workouts, and shopping, which you could never get away with if your Frog and its passenger had been with you. Your phone calls and emails to your buddies will also be uninterrupted by poopy diapers. When your baby begins to teethe, you will count down the minutes until you can escape to the sanctity of your wail-free office. And, most importantly, you will never have to ask your husband permission to buy another pair of shoes—after all, you're back at work and you deserve to indulge!

Sisterly Adjustments at Home and Work

It's all about efficiency. The faster you crank out your work, the quicker you can escape Alcatraz. Of course, it's all at the expense of your therapeutic bitching time. Remember how you used to obsess about food? The good news is that most **Sisters** who go back to work report that they become even skinnier than they were before becoming Possessed because between working and taking care of a child, they have no time to eat or even think about food. The bad news is that most **Sisters** are so tired and short on time that they don't have as much time to primp, so they become a bit skinny-shabby (not the same thing as shabby-chic, we're afraid).

Priorities, or should we say realities, will change. Remember when you used to drag yourself into the office with those big-black circles under your eyes after being up all night having sex? Now you will have the same big black circles, but they will be there as a result of being up all night with the wailing product of sex. If you have the choice between sleeping an extra thirty seconds or applying concealer, you will pick the sleep. And if you have to choose between accompanying your child to music class on a Saturday morning or getting your brows waxed and highlights touched up, guess who turns into a monobrow blonde with a black streak down her part?

On the home front, we regret to inform you that despite the fact that you are working as much as your husband, it is still the female, and the female alone, who seems to wind up in charge of *all* childcare and most household duties. We hate to break it to you, but better you hear it from us. If you assign any man the simple tasks of straightening up, taking care of the baby, and preparing a simple dinner all at once, smoke will start to come out of his ears and his circuits will short. You can try to even up the score, however, by delegating some of the less than desirable tasks one at a time, like taking out the garbage, followed by unclogging the drains that are backed up from your post-partum hair loss. If all else fails, some serious and routine retail therapy will reward you for all you do, oh Super Mommy-**Sister**.

Pumping and Practicing Law

If a **Sister** is still nursing when she returns to work, she will need to lug along her electric pump to the office. If you have never done this before, the thought of whipping out your boobs in the workplace will likely give you the heebie-jeebies, but trust us—all modesty will be forever lost after giving birth. We also note that most Y-Factors would rather stick #2 pencils in their eyeballs than acknowledge anything that has to do with feeding a baby from your booby, so don't even try to explain to your male boss why you keep your door locked for ten minutes a day.

The pumping and practicing stories we collected ran the gamut. One **Sister** told us that after she pumped, she would transport her milk to the firm's fridge in one of those insulated black cases. One day one of her male colleagues teased her for bringing her lunch to work in a kid's lunchbox. When she opened up the case to show him her baby food, he sprinted out of the kitchen faster than if he had seen anthrax.

A few words of advice on this delicate topic. First, whatever you do, make sure you cover yourself up while pumping, even if you work on the top floor of a high-rise building. More than one has reported pumping with her shirt wide open only to discover the window washer staring right back at her bare breasts. If you are on a certain pumping schedule, try not to miss a date with your plastic apparatus. It will only result in engorged breasts and milk-stained shirts (so don't forget to add nursing pads to your list of desk-drawer necessities).

Finally, just because you are pumping doesn't mean you can't bill. **Sisters** have reported that some of their most productive conference calls have occurred while their nipples were being stretched to the floor. (Of course, we don't recommend this practice in the case of video conferencing.)

The Nanny Gig

Unless your family members are willing to care for your baby (yeah, right), returning to work also means the added stress of hiring help to watch your new bundle of joy. Because your hours are irregular even on a good day, your best option is to hire a private babysitter. Believe us when we tell you that the candidates walking through your door are a far cry from Mary Poppins. So where do you find a governess for your princess? Best place is the **Sister** network. Nothing better than hiring another's former nanny who is no longer needed. After all, such a nanny has not only met the high standards set by another obsessive **Sister**, but also understands and can deal with having an anal-retentive perfectionistic boss.

While your husband will vote in favor of the hot Swedish nanny, you do, in fact, have three options.

- *Young Nannies.* These spring chickens are either single or have young children (often born fairly early in life). Upside: energetic and malleable. Downside: inexperienced, mildly flaky, and possibly irresponsible.
- *Mature Nannies.* These middle-aged women have years of experience and grown children. Upside: experienced and knowledgeable. Downside: set in their ways and may be opinionated.
- *Grandma Nannies.* These elderly women have children, grandchildren, and even great grandchildren. Upside: mature, calm, and experienced. Downside: unenergetic, opinionated, and a workers' compensation claim waiting to happen.

Despite the modest amount of money you pay them for changing your child's poopies, you will be surprised to discover that oftentimes they are better dressed and jeweled than you are. One **Sister** even confessed to borrowing her nanny's styling jacket that she had forgotten to take home over the weekend. Another told us that when she spied on her nanny to make sure she was taking good care of her little princess, she found the nanny spending three times her weekly paycheck on designer clothes on Fifth Avenue, all while pushing the little princess in the Frog.

Another weird phenomenon that **Sisters** encounter in nanny world is the strange interpersonal interaction between you and your nanny. While your nanny is your employee, she is also responsible for the well-being of your most precious asset. As such, you can't haze her like you would a junior associate and you will in fact feel somewhat beholden to her. After all, if you lose her, you will have the added stress of finding a replacement nanny. These handcuffs, of course, manifest with great force in the gift-giving arena. **Sisters** consistently report that their nannies received bigger and better Christmas gifts than anyone else in their families, including their own children.

The good news is that most **Sisters** love their nannies and think of them as part of their families. The bad news is that the nannies they speak so fondly of are not their first nannies. One last word about the nanny gig. Although child care is oftentimes paid for by both parents, a nanny who goes AWOL is almost always deemed to be exclusively the female's problem. Thus, you must be prepared with a backup plan, because your darling husband probably won't have one.

The Working Mommy Trump Card

While the Preggers Trump Card (PTC) was your get out of jail free card with respect to work, your Working Mommy Trump Card (WMTC) will serve the same purpose with respect to nonwork obligations. Have no idea what's going on in the world and no time to read the newspaper? Invoke the WMTC and change the subject.

Too tired to go to your Great Aunt Matilda's 90th birthday party? The WMTC will buy you the evening off. Wearing two different shoes to work? The WMTC excuses you from fashion *faux pas*. Don't worry, in 18 years when Junior is in college, you can watch the news, become a social butterfly, and coordinate all of your outfits. But until you get to that point, just invoke the WMTC.

Mommy Guilt

If you are Catholic, your priest will give it to you. If you are Jewish, your mother (or any other member of your family, for that matter) will give it to you. And if you are a **Sister** going back to work, your perfect little baby will (unintentionally) dole it out in droves. It's that powerful weapon that can just about crush your day—guilt.

All **Sisters**—even those who love their job and would never give a second thought to becoming a SAHM—feel the mommy-guilt at some point. When you first go back to work, it will nearly kill you. But over time, that nasty feeling will subside and after awhile your Gross Rationalization Disorder will make you believe that your nanny is indeed more functional than you are and therefore Junior is actually better adjusted than if you had stayed home.

Variations on the Full-Time Gig

Most high achieving **Sisters** admit that it's difficult, if not impossible, to ride with the breaks on. Because most of us can't do anything in moderation, we don't feel like we can do a good job if we work anything less than full-time (or at least less than our fellow associates). And while many of us change this mindset after having kiddies, our options to do anything less than full-time (at least outside of the inhouse counsel/government route) are somewhat limited.

In theory, you would think that in professions where you bill your time, it should be easy to reduce your hours by practicing part-time (working fewer than seventy hours weeks) or flex-time (working variable hours at times that are most convenient to you), or by job sharing (sharing your seventy-hour weeks with a co-worker) because the firm can simply prorate your compensation based on your hours. In reality, however, it's not such a simple equation. Because, for many of us, this issue is pivotal to our decision about whether or not to reenter Sisterhood, indulge us in our ad nauseum lawyerly dissection of the issue.

The issue of juggling work and family is so integral to Sisterly life that an entire organization has been created to collaborate on ways to make it work. Check out **Flextimelawyers.com** for more information.

From the law firm's perspective, embracing a fully disclosed formal flexible work arrangement policy (as opposed to secretive *ad hoc* policies which are all too common these days) is a good thing for several reasons.

- *Cost Savings.* According to a recent study [23], a firm loses approximately $200,000 in training and recruiting costs when it loses a second year associate. Imagine the cost when it loses a midlevel associate, the time at which many of us TTC and, coincidentally, finally become profitable to the firm. Some firms take the position that it costs more to hire part-time associates because the firm must pay the same costs for a part-timer's overhead (*i.e.*, your insurance, office, or secretary) as that of a full-time revenue generating machine. In contrast, we believe that the correct analysis is not to compare the cost of a full-time associate to a part-time associate, but to compare the cost of losing a full-time associate altogether (*i.e.*, $200,000+ in training) versus the *de minimus* extra overhead, if any, associated with allowing the full-time associate to cut down to part-time hours. [24]

- *Associate Good Will.* Sisters who do go part-time tell us that they feel more committed and willing (not to mention efficient) to go that extra mile for a firm that is willing to be flexible and accommodating.

■ *Client Relationships.* Most clients, who typically have more progressive human resources policies than law firms, want to hire firms that share their work philosophy.[25] Moreover, with nearly 50% of inhouse attorneys being women, law firms can only benefit if they are able to retain senior women who are only willing to work on a reduced schedule. Most clients would prefer to continue their relationship with a part-time associate they have been working with for eight years than pay the costs to get a new full-time associate up-to-speed on their business.

■ *Recruiting and PR.* The existence of a formal flexible work policy is emblematic of a progressive firm, which gives law school **Sister** recruits (even the ones that hate rugrats at the time) the warm fuzzies. Just look at the positive press that *Arnold & Porter* and *Morrison & Foerster* received when they were the first two law firms in history to appear on the *100 Best Places for Working Mothers* list published by *Working Mother*.[26] Flexible work schedules may also be helpful in minimizing female attrition rates—statistics that most large firms hide from recruits like the Holy Grail.

Despite all of these benefits, there are still hurdles that part-time attorneys face.

■ *Client Demands.* Many clients expect (and pay for) round-the-clock services. Moreover, if a deal is closing or a trial is set on your hallowed day-off, you will be expected to forego *The Wiggles* concert.

■ *Stigma.* Many of us believe that there is a stigma associated with part-time work—that people will think that we can't really be committed if we don't give 200% of ourselves. While nothing (absent a lobotomy) will convince a TesTy otherwise, we believe that this stigma will be overcome in time, as part-time **Sisters** prove that they can do the work just as well (and perhaps even more efficiently) than their full-time brethren.

- *Advancement.* Although in the past, many of us were cast-aside on the mommy-track once we went part-time, many big firms are now offering full equity partnership opportunities to part-timers. It may take a little longer to get there, but most Sisters report that having the extra time to spend time with their children is worth it. Part-time Sisters who have overcome such barriers report that they made themselves invaluable to either the firm or a specific client.

- *Defining Part-Time.* Surely you've heard the complaint that *I'm paid a part-time salary to work forty hours a week* coupled with the phrase *so part-time lawyering doesn't work.* We would posit that this argument may be purely semantic. So long as you're working fewer hours than your peers and you're happier (or at least a little less stressed out), the system does work, even if it isn't entirely fair.[27]

There is no doubt that successful part-time arrangements take a lot of effort even at the most enlightened firms. In order to truly make it work, you will need to understand, appreciate, and accept that as a lawyer, you are a service provider. In order to thrive in this line of work as a part-time or flex-time attorney, there are two words define success—*accessibility* and *reactivity.* If you can be reached and can react in a timely manner to a client's requests, even on your time out of the office, it shouldn't matter whether or not you are in the office at any given time. With our virtual *law on-the-go* devices—email, cell phones, faxes, laptops and Crackberries—at our disposal, doing the part-time gig should be easier and more accepted than ever.

One last thing before we try to be funny again—if you have a part-time deal that is working out, go public and become an evangelist for the system! It is only in this way that we, or at the very least our mini-Sisters, can perhaps claim that *you can have it all.*

Juggling All the Balls

Juggling all the balls in the air will be the single most difficult part of your day. You will constantly feel like you can't be a good mommy and you can't be a good lawyer. Oftentimes, you will walk out of the house and reach for your wallet in your bag only to pull out a diaper. You will zone out during a conference call because in your head you were singing *I'm a Little Teapot*. We all do it—you need to cut yourself some slack and surrender. This is not one day, but the rest of your life **Sister**, so try to simplify and eliminate the nonessentials (which sadly may include mani's and pedi's).

THE FINAL ASSESSMENT

It seems that Mommies who choose to remain in the **Sisterhood** will have their good days and bad days. On good days, your nanny will show up on time and your smiling baby will throw you kisses as you sashay out the door. You will put in eight hours of challenging, but only moderately stressful billables, and you will run to the gym or do a bit of shopping during lunch. You will get out the door at a reasonable time to return home to the same goo goo-ing, happy baby you left in the morning. You will be proud that you are putting all of those years of education to use and are a valuable member of the working society. On these days, you will also feel pleased to be setting such an inspiring example for your son or daughter.

And then there are the REAL days, which may look something like this.

Your darling six-month old wakes you up at 5:30 a.m. eager to eat and play, even though you were up to 2 a.m. finishing your brief. By 6 a.m., the dog starts to jump all over you and baby. Half-asleep, you shove baby in a carrier strapped to your chest and drag the dog and baby for a brisk walk. Husband is still sleeping because he has an incurable case of HINDS.

Upon return to the apartment, you discover husband has done the disappearing act to go to work while you were walking the dog. You stare at the clock, and with each passing second, you pray to the nanny-gods that yours shows up today. Nanny shows up 15 minutes late due to the invariable train delay, and you sprint to work.

You work like a madwoman to finish up your research, not even stopping to web surf or talk to Bingin' and Bitchin' Buddies. You bolt home because you are terrified of being late again and pissing off the nanny—train delays are not an excuse. You enter the front door to the warm embrace of no one, except the dog. Baby starts wailing. Dog starts barking.

As you still have not completely transitioned into mommy-mode, you neurotically keep checking your Crackberry (hoping it's water and bubble bath proof) to make sure you didn't get fired while simultaneously singing Elmo and Rubber Ducky 6,000 times to baby in the bathtub.

You finally fall into a coma-like state on the couch, where the only thing you can do is curl into your darling hubby's arms and stare at pictures in In-Style Magazine (and wish you had time to buy ANYTHING). All of a sudden, your husband takes your hand, gives you a kiss and says, "Honey, you are the kindest, smartest, most beautiful woman in the world, and we have a perfect baby. There's nothing I want more than another child who is exactly like you and Baby #1."

And thus, the whole bloody cycle starts all over again.

■ ■ ■

8

Sisterly Secrets

–simultaneously lawyering and living a full life–

If there's one consistent theme you'll hear about practicing law time and time again, it's how stressed out and time deprived we **Sisters** are as a result of our jobs. The source of the stress tends to be fourfold. First, as a result of billable hour requirements, many of us obsessively keep track of all of our hours to date, constantly running Einstein-like calculations of how many more hours it will take to reach our minimum yearly quotas. Second, when you work for someone else (*i.e.*, partners with unreasonable demands), your life is in not your own and you feel completely out of control. This results in your having panic attacks after finally hitting your pillow at 1 a.m., when you start thinking *I didn't get enough work done today. What if someone gives me an emergency assignment and I don't have time to finalize this brief?*

Third, and perhaps most significantly, your client's fate is in your hands and you don't want to screw up someone else's affairs. There are hundreds of little things to remember (like discovery deadlines) and there's always another argument that can be made or researched on behalf of your client. Basically, you feel like your job is never done, and even when it is, you could have done it better.

Lastly, much of what we do in law is extremely time sensitive (*i.e.*, always urgent), yet at the same time tremendously laborious. Everyone wants something yesterday that in reality would take until next week to thoroughly complete.

The result of these intense pressures is that many of us never leave our office and even when we do, it's only in the physical sense. Sometimes, however, even physically leaving the office becomes more stressful than staying put. There's the chance that you'll miss an important client or partner call or worse yet, be unreachable if someone urgently needs the answer to a critical question and only you know that answer. Once your memory of what it's like to have a life outside of work fades, your office may not seem like the worst vacation destination anymore.

As a result, some of us get so wrapped up with work that we completely lose touch with reality. Take, for example, the eleven-page memorandum the battered associates at Clifford Chance delivered to the firm after it came in dead last in the 2002 American Lawyer Associate Survey. The infamous memorandum spelled out exactly what the associates thought was wrong with the place and offered some suggestions for how their quality of life could be improved. The memo included among other things:

- *put plates and utensils in pantries at the firm, so that people working late can avoid eating out of containers;*
- *set up a recreation room with a TV;* and,
- *provide concierge service for dry-cleaning.*[28]

Of course, had these associates not been brainwashed into thinking that working 24/7 was the norm, their wish-list may have contained requests like:

- *I'd like to eat dinner at home with my family;*
- *I'd like to watch TV in my own living room at night;* or,
- *I'd like to get out of this place before 7 p.m. some nights so I could actually make it to pick up at my own dry cleaning.*[29]

It should be no mystery why so many lawyers are unhappy and unhealthy.[30] We work too much and then we become convinced that this is normal behavior. Every hour spent working is one less hour spent doing something pleasurable, but soon we forget what *pleasurable* means. And don't think for a second that, no matter how hard you work and how high you bill, anyone (besides your mother) will ever tell you to take a break, go home, plan a vacation, or do something decadent and nonlaw-related once in a while.

That's where we come in. We're here to tell you that you need to find ways to de-stress, whether its blowing off steam while you are chained to your desk, taking breaks, or making the most of your time away from the office. So relax and join us in a very nonwork-related journey.

CHAINED TO YOUR DESK

Sometimes **Sisters** just can't tear themselves away from the office because they are swamped with work and imminent deadlines. Other times, they hang out when they really don't have to be there because they buy into Dilbert's theory that appearances are everything. In other words, you believe that doing *face time* in the office and looking busy even if you're not must somehow be important to your career. If you find yourself stuck in the office for either of the above reasons, there are still three therapies, so to speak, you can employ to blow off steam while chained to your desk.

Your Electronic Therapist (*aka* your Computer)

Pass by any lawyer's office on any given day, and if they are not on the phone or with a visitor, chances are they will be deep in concentration hacking away at their computers. Are they always working on the deal of the century? Of course not! Let's face it, preparing your profile for an online dating service looks pretty much the same as revising provisions of a zillion dollar contract. For many of us, the electronic therapist is the best form of relaxing and taking a brain-break. Because most of us are glued to the computer the vast majority of the workday, high-speed access to the world outside the office has become the "digital equivalent of a smoking break."[31] Let's consider how **Sisters** use the magic box to *de-stress*.

EMAIL

For many of us working long hours, email is the last vestige of communication we have to the outside world. Many of us live for the welcoming *ping* or instant message that so rudely interrupts our real work. If we haven't received any e-candy in over a half-hour, we start neurotically pressing the *refresh* button to make sure we haven't missed anything from our friends or boytoys. For some of us, we can live two offices away from a Bingin' and Bitchin' Buddy, yet most of our conversations may be had over the magic box.

Besides serving as a critical distraction to boring document review, **Sisters** love email because it offers completely neutral delivery of any message, even from the most evil partner. Why? Because it is generally devoid of human emotion.

Your computer and its network are company property and can be easily monitored by the firm's techno-geeks. Therefore, it may be advisable to open a free email account and use it for all personal emails.

Yelling, stomping, and degrading tones are undeliverable. It's virtually impossible to detect the mood of the sender and/or tone of the message in most cases (the exception being when you insert those little yellow smiley faces at the bottom of your emails to friends) even though you may spend half a day obsessively dissecting every word to try to figure out what was really meant by the sender. And from the sender side, of course, what better way to appease your passive aggressive tendencies than to give the boot to Mr. Mediocrity by advising him in writing of your unavailability to see him in the next few decades.

Email is also a handy enabler of many of our **Sisterly** disorders. Our Perfection Disorder is fostered by the email routine. We type, review, revise seven times, save as draft, review in a few hours when we've had a chance to think about things, and then send, but only after checking three times to make sure each recipient is correct. Of course, by the time we hit *send*, all that is left is the subject line because we're so neurotic about our written words (which can't be taken back or denied) being misinterpreted, printed, and shown to the rest of the world.

Nothing could be better for our Anal-Retentive Disorder than to have the ability to file, subfile, cleanup, delete, and save to archives all important information for eternity right inside the magic box, with no color-coated sticky-tabs needed!

And finally, we don't even need to tell you how we play the Multitasking Madness game with email. We can have a blow out fight (and win, of course) with our boyfriends *via* instant messaging all the while participating on an overseas conference call, drafting schedules to a deal document, and doing isometric stomach crunches. Oftentimes, the mere banging away on the keyboard in a message to your girlfriend about how inconsiderate your husband may be acting (with the most egregious behavior always spelled out in capital letters) is therapeutic in and of itself because it takes four times longer to type the story than to tell it. By the time you hit *send*, your anxiety has dissipated.

Although e-therapy has its pluses, it's possible that at some point, due to our total reliance on email as our sole source of communication, we will lose the ability to talk to people in person. Any method of communication that doesn't allow us to quash our emotions and draft, redraft, save draft, and revisit later to re-edit before delivering will eventually scare the B-Jesus out of us.

Surfing

Could there be anything better than typing any word in the whole English language into Saint Google and getting a million hits instantaneously? Whether it's looking for a piece of information or just feeding our tired heads some brain candy, **Sisters** spend more time than they are willing to admit surfing the Web for periodic stress relief.

From the comfort of your office chair, you can check your stock portfolio (which is generally closely followed by a Niemanmarcus.com visit if the market it up), plan your next vacation, read the recipe of the day on Epicurious.com, and watch a movie trailer, all while looking like you are working on a very important project. There is no doubt that the World Wide Web is God's gift to **Sisters** and other repressed, office-chained, tortured soles.

E-SHOPPING

Did you know that 59% of the $45 billion in U.S. Web purchases in 2002 originated from the workplace, compared with 37% from home and 4% from schools?[32] Even more shocking is that online shopping seems to begin with an average workday, jump noticeably around 10:00 a.m. and steadily build up through noon. It drops between noon and one p.m. (the typical lunch break) and then rises again between 3 p.m. and 5 p.m. as the workday ends (for nonlawyers, that is).[33] Of course, women account for more than half of all online shoppers and we suspect that the **Sister** population accounts for a healthy chunk of these buyers.[34]

Since most of us don't have time to hit the stores during the week (and for many of us, during the weekends), there really isn't any time left in the day to shop outside the office. For us, there is no better therapy than spending our hard earned greenbacks without leaving the comfort of our offices. A few simple clicks of a button (usually occurring at the tail end of two hours of Web window shopping and price comparisons) and a thousand dollars later

($300 of which are overnight delivery fees) gets you the fruits of your labor delivered right to your LASS-producing chair.

Your Live Therapists (*aka* Bitching)

As much as the magic box can fulfill most of our therapeutic needs, there are times when you crave interaction with a warm body who has a pulse. Sometimes, there's only one way to deal with the stressful practice of law without internally combusting: bitching, complaining, kvetching (Yiddish for black-belt, master complaining), grumbling, nagging, nitpicking, and whining about how much everything sucks to anyone who will listen. For many of us, nothing is more therapeutic than storming into a colleague's office, closing the door, and venting (and for many of us in the early years, crying) about the BBQ who just chewed you up and spit you out. The scenario usually goes something like this.

> You run into your Bingin' and Bitchin' Buddy's office and threaten to: *(1)* quit; *(2) give up your personal trainer; (3) sell your Hamptons share; and, (4) open a flower shop. After consuming 300 M&M's, you are calmly reminded by your friend that: (1) you are florally challenged; (2) because all of the other people in your Hamptons house are lawyers, there is a transferability restriction on your share; and, (3) without a personal trainer, you would have three LASSes instead of one. Before you know it, you have calmed down, regained your composure and even discussed how you may go about tackling the memo from hell (thereby rendering the entire bitching session billable).*

If all of your top therapists are out of the office, you may venture outside your four walls. Pick up the phone and call any of your Sisters at other firms to commiserate. If things get really bad, you may wish to turn to the most sympathetic of all therapists—your mother. Although she knows how perfect you are and can do no wrong, keep in mind that using her services may come at a price. Even after you recover from your meltdown, she will never forgive the perpetrator of your sorrows and nag you for the next ten years to leave the firm or go back to med school.

Sidebar

If you run out of candidates to listen to your complaints, never fear—you can vent to total strangers on workorspoon.com. This website was invented by a gentleman by the name of Spoonman. One day while he was getting ready to go to work he stopped in the kitchen and grabbed a spoon. He looked into the mirror and asked himself, "Which is more painful; going to work or gouging out one of my eyes with this spoon?" Turns out his feelings were shared by many friends, all of whom wanted to bitch and complain about their work. If Spoonman sounds a little eccentric for your tastes, also consider bitching to other associates on greedyassociates.com or other working mommies from your city on urbanbaby.com (with no surprises that the New York urbanbaby.com chat room has by far the best bitchin').

ESCAPING ALCATRAZ

Once you've finished your work, dropped a cool $1,000 e-shopping, and finished bitchin' with all your buddies, you should consider taking a break—whether it's just stepping away, going to lunch, leaving for the night, or the motherload of breaks: going on vacation. As we mentioned earlier, many of us are afraid to take breaks because we fear that Big Brother is watching us with the expectation that we should be working 24/7. While you shouldn't leave the office if you really have work to complete, there is no reason to hang around just because you fear that the insecure Affable Alligators and Bubble Associates will make snide remarks that you work *part-time* if they see you leaving at 6 p.m. In this section, we'll discuss **sisterly** tricks of the trade for executing the magical disappearing act without anyone catching on.

The Short Break

Short breaks, even in the worst sweatshops, are generally accepted. After all, taking a few minutes to relax your mind and walk around generally makes you more productive. Besides, if we didn't take at least a few short breaks throughout the day, we'd wind up filing for disability due to incontinence and bladder infections. Short breaks are also used to binge, bitch, freshen up, caffeinate, and hydrate.

No special preparations are needed for the short break, because they last no more than .25 of an hour (theoretically, at least), which everyone generally backs out of their billable day anyway.

The Midday Break

Generally speaking, employers are not opposed to their workhorses fueling or hydrating during the workday, so there are no special preparations needed if you're just going out to grab a carb-free wrap at the deli and eat it at your desk.

However, the extended lunchtime break (defined as anything longer than ½ hour) is a whole other story. While marathon-eating escapades do occur from time to time during the extended lunchtime break, this break usually has nothing whatsoever to do with food. **Sisters** typically use this midday work reprieve for shopping, interviewing with kinder and gentler firms, waxing, highlights, mani's/pedi's, doctor (and shrink) visits, or running home to visit baby, pet, or pillow.

Of course, those blessed with an in-house workout facility or nearby gyms swear by the workout break. Most of us are

Food is actually a sign of weakness when you are in negotiation sessions that span the lunch hour—the first party to suggest *Let's order in*—is clearly not as focused on getting the job done.

too darn tired to get our LASS out of bed in the morning to hit the gym. By the end of our working days, we are again too darn tired to whip out the running shoes and besides, the gym is probably closed by the time some of us depart the office for the day. If you can manage to escape for at least 1.5 hours, there's nothing better to revive you than getting the heart rate up with something other than coffee or chocolate.

Armed with your Crackberry and cell phone, you really can't miss any emergencies either. Many **Sisters** even claim that they can bill time while at the gym by rehearsing oral arguments in their head while climbing the Stairmaster (we neither approve or disapprove of this billing practice, but it seems to make sense).

So what kind of special preparations do you need for the extended lunch break? First off, you'll need a cover person, who is usually your secretary. You will need to brainwash this person to tell anyone who asks for you that "Ms. **Sister** just stepped away from her desk, may I take a message." You then provide her with your cell and Crackberry information and tell her not to contact you unless one of very few important people call. Some **Sisters** are so desperate to sneak out for an undetected workout that they will forego wearing their coat out the door and freeze their LASSes off sprinting to the gym or the car.

In our humble opinions, 1.5 hours is probably the minimum time you need to get in a decent workout, commute, shower, and grab something to eat at your desk. In a crunch, you can cut down on shower time by doing a low-impact non-sweaty activity. Yes, it's sort of gross, but there is a reason God created deodorant, powder, and perfume.

You also want to make your office appear as if you just stepped out for a short break. Keep your computer and lights on, scatter paperwork, books, and files all over your desk, and whatever you do, DO NOT TIDY UP. If you are worried that your two-hour tryst will unnecessarily send out the search dogs, whip out a stale bagel from the conference room, fill up your coffee cup, and go on your merry way.

If you're doing retail therapy, you should leave all of your goodies in your car. If, however, you don't drive, you will need to make friends with someone who sits on a different floor of your building or the doorman so you can conveniently drop off your purchases and return to your work-station empty-handed. If you're going waxing, don't forget to take along some powder or foundation to hide the tell-tale pink lines between your eyebrows and above your lip and try to avoid walking bowlegged if you're returning from a bikini wax.

The workout break requires a bit more preparation detail. Since you don't want to be caught escaping Alcatraz lugging your gym bag, consider renting a locker at the gym. When you success-fully return from the gym undetected, you may be faced with yet another dilemma—where do you file your smelly workout clothes? Some **Sisters** designate a hamper drawer (which is right next to the shoe drawer), but please, don't forget to empty it out every week or the smell will eventually overtake your office.

The Daily Exodus

Even the most dedicated workaholics tend to vanish without a trace when it's time to go home for the night. After all, drive by any high rise building in the wee hours of a Sunday morning and take note that the majority of the office lights are still on. Do you really think so many worker bees are plugging away on their computers at that insane hour? Chances are, the lights are on, but nobody is home.

Most **Sisters** understand that preparation for this type of break is much more extensive than the other breaks because it's a bigger time commitment away from billing (*i.e.*, at least six hours). Even amateurs know that at a minimum, you will need to cover your desk (and client chairs, as indicated) with one or more of the following items prior to your departure.

- *Work*. Scatter paperwork on the top of your desk so it looks as if you are in the middle of preparing something very important. Sprinkling a few used legal pads, sticky notes, and highlighters into the mix can't hurt either.
- *Books*. Grab your most frequently used books and open them up on your desk.
- *Briefcase*. At some point in your legal career, someone like your Grandma Edna will buy you one of those ugly skinny briefcases that holds no more than a small sticky note pad. You wanted to return or regift it, but alas, it was lovingly monogrammed with your initials. Don't fret. Here's your chance to use it.

Seasoned **Sisters** may invest in a more sophisticated system and resort to Decoy Escape **Sister** Kit (DESK) tools. Your DESK tools should be hidden in a drawer next to the shoe and hamper drawers and kept under lock and key until you are ready to depart, and then they are scattered on your desktop. The most basic DESK tools include the following items.

If you have access to a *lit-bag* (lawyerese for those big black rolling box briefcases), you may also want to consider throwing some files in it, leaving the top open and displaying it next to your desk chair. If you look closely, you will note that these unsightly black tombs will remain untouched in the exact same position in lawyers' offices for days, weeks, months, and even years at a time.

- *DESK Purse.* This is not the $500 Louis Vuitton you guard with your life. We're talking a Chinatown Louis fakeout or even a beaten up old purse from last season that you wouldn't be caught dead holding. Even the most obtuse Y-Factor knows that no **Sister** would ever leave the office without her purse, no matter how ugly and out of style it is.
- *DESK Keys.* Make a copy of the office key (which you will inevitably need in a pinch because all disorganized **Sisters** waste at least an hour a day ripping apart their office looking for their keys) and throw it on a big key chain. Grab all of those random *I have no idea what this goes to* keys sitting in the junk drawer at home and attach to the keychain.
- *DESK Jacket.* Keep an old jacket on hand and drape it over your chair or on the back of your door.

If you work with snoopy Bubble Associates and want to guarantee that the powers that be believe you're available late into the evening, consider the Deluxe DESK tool set, which includes all of the above, plus the following:

- *DESK Bait.* Just as you do for Santa Claus on Christmas Eve, leave a plate of food and an empty soda can. One word of caution, however, choose your foods wisely. Last thing you want is to come back in the morning and smell spoiled tuna fish accompanied by *las cucarachas* milling about.
- *DESK Perfume.* Spill a little of the cheap samples (forced on you by those pushy salespeople while shopping on your extended lunch break) on top of your radiators to convince all the snoopers' senses that you must have just left the room.

Armed with your DESK tools, make a run for it! One more thing—to avoid getting snagged on the way out the door, employ the **Sisterly** trick of walking out with a cell phone to your ear pretending to have a serious client call all the way to the front door.

Of course, most Newbies don't have any client contact whatsoever, but keep it in your bag of DESK tools for a later date.

Vacation

Even if you master the art of the short break, lunch break, and overnight break, a **Sister** cannot survive on mini-respites alone. Twelve percent of the American work force forego vacation annually because they have too much work to do.[35] Our advice? Use your vacation! It will be your panacea and salvation in many cases. Many **Sisters** we know live to vacation and vacation to live.

Since we generally have a low tolerance for boredom, nothing but the most exotic, adventurous, and luxurious holidays will do. No sooner do we return to post-vacation hell than we start researching our next journey. If you plan one of these whirlwind trips, however, you should be warned that you risk the chance of not being able to go if you get pulled onto a time-sensitive deal or case. Many firms actually have a policy to cover your cancellation costs in such cases, so these firms will try their hardest to set their vacation birds free (so long as you carry your cell phone and Crackberry, of course).

As an aside, our sources tell us that the Crackberry does not work in cold climates, European countries, and while flying at altitudes of 30,000 feet. Perhaps this would explain why so many Crackberry-using **Sisters** vacation in Alaska, Italy, and Costa Rica.

Preparation required for the mega-break? Besides giving your employer advanced notice of your vacation dates and crash dieting to fit into your thong bikini, there's really nothing you need to do. It's the one break where appearances simply don't matter. Turn off your lights, shut down your computer, and enjoy your time off. When you finally dig yourself out of post-vacation hell, just remember, the best way to cure your post-vacation blues is to plan your next trip.

AFTER THE GREAT ESCAPE

Once you successfully escape Alcatraz, assuming you're not on one of your fabulous holidays (as the Euros like to say), what can you do to maximize your time away from the office, de-stress, and delude yourself into thinking that you have a life? Although we should do it more, we have a hard time doing nothing. For most of us, peace, quiet, and solitude drives us mad after about ten minutes. Let's visit a few of the stress-releases Sisters enjoy the most.

Exercise

The trouble with exercise is that, like eating, Sisters can't seem to do it in moderation. On one hand, just as we subscribe to the *no pain, no gain* theory at the office, our workouts are subject to the same torturous standard. This means we don't feel fulfilled unless we submit ourselves to hour-long, high-impact cardio workouts where our heart rate tops 170 beats per minute and sweat drips out of every pore of our body. We can't just jog three miles—we have to train for marathons.

On the other hand, if we suspect that we have anything less than an hour to kill ourselves with a ball-busting regime, it's not even worth it to waste our precious time. Similarly, if we don't stick to our new no-carb under–1,200 calorie fantasy diet (*i.e.*, we binge on a giant size bag of Hershey kisses in the morning, indulge in a greasy burger and fries at noon, and slurp down a Carmel Macchiato at 3 p.m.), all the working out in the world will not burn off those calories, so why bother.

Canine and Feline Therapy

What better way to help you de-stress than to know that you have a furry companion who loves you unconditionally, doesn't talk back, and thinks you are the nicest, smartest, most loving person that ever walked on the face of this earth? Although it may be scary to be responsible for keeping something alive other than yourself (and you barely manage to do that sometimes), **Sisters** say there's nothing like it.

CANINE THERAPY

A simple lick, bark, snuggle, or wag of the tail can brighten even your worst day. It's blatantly clear that few men can ever live up to this perfect furry lover. Y-factor maintenance involves mind games, sexual needs, and battles over the remote controls. All your snuggly boarder wants from you is a scratch on his tummy and a toss of the tennis ball.

FELINE THERAPY

Unfortunately, your authors are dog lovers, so for us, cats just seem like fat, unhappy animals who do nothing all day except sleep, shed, eat Friskies, purr, and hurl fur balls. When we interviewed **Sister** feline lovers, they claimed that these quiet, unobtrusive felines are one of the best companions with whom a busy **Sister** can share her life. Why? From what we have heard, cats won't chew up your expensive Manolo shoes or defecate all over your house. Morris the cat seems to be con-

As an aside, we were also fascinated to discover that unlike us, cats are the masters of self-restraint. No matter how tempting the gallon bag of Friskies looks, cats will only eat when they are hungry.

tent with a giant bowl of Friskies buffet and a litter box. So, why would a Sister choose a cat over a dog? Have you ever heard of anyone suing a cat owner for a cat bite?

Pampering

Nothing beats good old-fashioned pampering. The most basic form is probably the manicure/pedicure, where you can relax and kick back with the brain-candy magazines you can't bring yourself to buy at the grocery store checkout counter. Although none of us enjoy sitting in a nail salon surrounded by smelly feet and gnarly foot diseases, this is our oasis. And magically, no matter how fat or ugly we feel, a few coats of nail polish make us feel more like a princess.

While waxing is far from fun, it is part of a your total maintenance regime. And despite the fact that boiling wax chars your skin right before it (your skin, that is) is ripped off your body, some Sisters report that it can be weirdly relaxing.

Hobbies

No, taking out the trash and watching five hours of *Oprah* (thanks to Tivo, of course) are not hobbies. Sisters report that it is important for them to have things going on in their lives that are not work, boy, or narcissistic related activities (hard to believe there's anything outside of these things, right?). The problem is, practicing law tends to annihilate any scintilla of creative juice you may have once possessed.

Despite the odds, Sisters do report that they have found some satisfaction in taking classes in things as diverse as painting pottery (even though the finished piece looks like something our two-year-old child created); tennis (even though we can't keep the ball in the court); and, culinary cooking classes (even though we almost burn down our apartment making cherries jubilee). Sadly, we're usually so mediocre at all of these things that our interest peters out after the first few classes, and we are yet again hit by the brutal reality that we cannot give up our day jobs.

Professional (*i.e.*, expensive) Therapy

If you've tried everything we've suggested in this chapter and you're still a stressed-out mess, it may be time to hit the professional's couch. Whatever problems you had before starting therapy, however, may be multiplied by the stress you encounter when you can't make your sessions due to work-related emergencies (which occur daily).

Doesn't it seem a bit paradoxical, in any event, that Sisters, perhaps the most cynical people of any profession, would take someone else's blanket assertion, without seventeen authorities to back it up, as wholehearted gospel? Whatever these highly-paid listeners do, however, seems to be working. Or maybe we are just nostalgic for the Socratic method of our law school days—we long for the perpetual circular reasoning and illogical analysis in which we eventually wind up answering all of our questions ourselves anyway.

RELAX!

Don't say we didn't warn you about how overwhelmed you will feel when you embark on a career in our noble profession. But we trust that this chapter has provided you with hope that you can even out the good and bad days. Use your e-therapy, Bingin' and Bitchin' Buddies, DESK tools—whatever it takes—to try to stay sane in this insane practice of law. And even if you go insane, you can pay someone to tell you that you are sane, which is just as effective. Now that you are calm, cool, and collected, it's time to go back to substantive issues (which will drive you insane again).

■ ■ ■

Part III

One, Two, Buckle My Shoe:
Everything They Don't Teach Sisters
in Law School about Practicing Law

9

Strutting in Your New Shoes

-the nuts and bolts of practicing law-

W hat most **Sisters** don't realize at the beginning of their careers is that they are entering a slightly quirky and eccentric subculture of society (affectionately referred to herein as the *Beast*). In this chapter, we present you with our collected knowledge and stories about the unique methods in which we learn our trade (understanding the *Beast* within), generate revenues on behalf of our employers (appreciating the Queen *Beast*), and interact with others (socializing the *Beast*). Until you've lived it, it's nearly impossible to fully understand it. Nevertheless, we'll use our best efforts and invoke reasonable due diligence[36] to give you some pointers on what to expect while strutting around town in your new shoes.

UNDERSTANDING THE BEAST WITHIN

There are a number of tasks, duties, and challenges that you will encounter in your young and tender Newbie years. Many of these mundane responsibilities will insult your intelligence, intimidate, and frustrate you. In fact, there are very few rewarding moments in the initial months of practice. Take the following scenario.

In the six months you've been with the firm, you have collected a six-digit salary for summarizing six thousand pounds of deposition transcripts dating back to 1966. Although you're annoyed that you're not doing something more brainworthy, you actually start to look forward to the eight uninterrupted hours of mindless document review while carrying on intense conversations with your other Newbie Sisters *about which* Sex in the City *character you are most like (sadly, it's usually Miranda). In the middle of your 1,406th hour of billing to this same client, the unthinkable happens. Your phone rings. The caller ID reveals it's the BBQ. You immediately develop a partner paranoia-induced rash. Before you even have a chance to decide if you should answer it, she's in your office about to deliver the worst news of your life. Another associate just bit the dust (quit, not perished) minutes before he was to board a plane for a month-long stint in Nebraska for depositions in an unrelated contentious litigation matter. Handing you a one-way ticket to a state you haven't even thought about since fifth grade geography, she tells you to cancel your plans—indefinitely—and get ready to join the team.*

As she walks out of your office, sheer panic sets in. Why? Despite three grueling years of law school and six months at the firm, it suddenly dawns on you that you know absolutely nothing.

We have all felt that way and there's no need to despair. So how do Sisters become capable of actually contributing something of value? Join us through some of the trials and tribulations you can expect to encounter in the Newbie years on the journey to becoming a *real* lawyer.

Training

What kind of training does the office provide? Recognize the question? It's the one we all ask during the interview process. Unfortunately, the truth of the matter is that in law you learn by doing. Period. Problem is, it's impossible to *do* when you don't know what you're doing, particularly when clients are not too fond of paying for your training time or having mistakes incurred on their dime. One way or another, you eventually figure out what's going on. There seems to be four general methods of learning the ropes.

First, there's the *Learn and Burn Method*, whereby you are given limited or no direction at all. You will be handed a client file and told to *take care of it*. It's like putting on a blindfold and walking over a bed of hot coals in bare feet—no matter how careful you are, you will make painful mistakes and feel scarred for life.

Second, there's the *Me and My Shadow Method*, in which senior attorneys run the show and allow Newbies-in-training to observe the elders perform their magic (however unmagical it may appear). Other than completing mindless discrete tasks and pretending to be impressed by the senior attorneys' talents, Sisters trained in this manner do little more than develop LASS.

Third, there's the *Toil Away in Isolation Method*, which combines the worst from the two methods identified above. Specifically, the senior attorneys give Newbie Sisters no direction at all, and at the same time allow them free reign to do everything—from wading through a warehouse full of boxes in an effort to locate the word *material* to trying a case on their own.

And last but not least (and perhaps the best), is the *Mensching and Mentoring Method*. Call it heaven (or chocolate without calories). Training Sisters learn their craft from Saintly Mentors who treat them like their own child (and oftentimes even better). No question is dumb and no mistake is lethal. You work your way up from performing discrete tasks to becoming a major player. In fact, many plugging for partnership claim that their efforts are fruitless without a *promoter* (*i.e.*, a single partner who pushes for the Sister's career).

One word to the wise here—although many firms will assign you a *mentor* as part of the recruiting protocol, this person may remain as alien to you as the theory of relativity. Oftentimes, you will need to seek out a mentor whose style you would like to emulate or who is known to promote the development of his or her associates.

At the end of the day, while we all prefer heaven over hell (and ice cream over celery), after you have put in a few years and more than a few thousand hours, you will eventually learn your trade under any of these methods. And even if you don't find your menschy mentor, some of the best lawyers we know attribute their success to figuring out things the hard way in their early years.

Grunt Work

As a first-year associate (and at some firms, as a second- and third-year associate), you need to remember that you are the lowest person on the totem pole—in many cases, even lower than the secretaries and paralegals. You will need to understand and accept the fact that all grunt work will typically start and end with you. On one hand, the mundane, monkey like tasks will generate easy billable hours and make your days fly by. The bad news is that you will start to neurotically obsess that you are losing your marketability because you are not learning anything. Before you know it, you start to think that if your firm goes under, you have nothing to offer another employer and that you will certainly wind up as a bag lady on a park bench (precipitating the question, of course, of whether or not bag ladies have to repay their student loans).

Relax. We've all been there and believe us, it's no secret to anyone that you are paid to tab exhibits and cut and paste excerpts of everything in the early years.

Assignments

Typically, Newbies will be given discrete assignments by an assigning Attorney Senior Supervisor (the ASS) that are communicated in a variety of ways—from formal written memos to informal (and oftentimes incomprehensible) verbal orders. Many of us have worked for the passive-aggressive ASS, who will leave you a note on your chair (usually scribbled in their secret special shorthand code) or voicemail asking you to do this or that. You can read that note and listen to that voicemail about 4,000 times and still not have a bloody clue what the ASS wants. Solution? You must ask others who have worked for the ASS (even their secretaries can help out) what the hell he wants. Oftentimes, there is a partner-lingo that you can only learn by living in the respective ASS's world for a while, so don't waste your time trying to decipher it yourself.

Once you figure out the task, what next? There's a checklist of questions you need to tuck away in your overworked brain (somewhere in between the list of the hottest spring fashions and your favorite restaurants), and ask when confronted with a task.

WHAT IS THE DUE DATE?

Lawyers are notorious for shrugging their shoulders and nonchalantly responding, *in due course.* In any event, to avoid being labeled an irresponsible slacker if your interpretation of *due course* is different from that of the ASS, insist on a firm deadline. Unfortunately, oftentimes, the interpretation will be three days ago.

We would be remiss if we didn't point out that the number one complaint among Newbie Sisters is the false due date. The scenario looks something like this. After pulling three all-nighters researching and writing an emergency memorandum on the tax collateralization rules in Uruguay, you spot your memo, unread and collecting round coffee cup stains, sitting on the ASS's desk three weeks following its majestic delivery. Why does this happen if the partner knows the baby's true due date?

As ASSes ourselves, let us share our hypothesis about false due dates, as well as the invariable emergency project. First, lawyers are notoriously bad managers and most suffer from Delegation Deficit Disorder. Thus, they usually save doling out assignments until crisis mode sets in because the time and effort it takes to explain the assignment and subsequently edit Newbie work-product far exceeds the time it

It is worth mentioning that some very cynical Sisters claim that the true underpinnings of the false due date lie in the power tripping high that certain ASSes get out of grabbing you at 7:30 p.m. on a Friday night and killing your weekend with an unnecessary assignment due on Monday.

would take to do it themselves. Second, false due dates are the result of lawyers being perpetually swamped and disorganized. They never know when they will have time to review your work, so if they have a few minutes over the next few weeks to read it, they want to make sure it's ready and waiting at their fingertips.

Unfortunately, at the end of the day it's better to get your assignment to the ASS when they ask for it and not obsess over their rationale—just in case they really do need it yesterday.

DO YOU WANT A WRITTEN OR ORAL RESPONSE?

Most of us would prefer to avoid IRAC and *ad nauseum* Bluebook citations[37] if they are not necessary. So save yourself the trouble by asking if the ASS just wants a quick answer or whether you must, in fact, produce the equivalent of a law review article.

Sidebar

Not the country, but even worse—IRAC is the draconian rule governing how one must write a legal memorandum in law school.

Issues: state the issue to be presented
Rule: state the rule of law that applies
Analysis: apply the rule of law to the facts of the case
Conclusion: sum up the answer to the issue presented

If written product is required, you should remember that while diarrhea of the mouth (*i.e.*, your gift for verbal persuasion) may assist you in getting your way with your family and friends, it does not fare well in the legal, written world.[38] Try to get to the point or heart of the issue with the most important arguments and authority first and remember that it's always about quality rather than quantity (unless we're talking about billables).

DO YOU HAVE ANY FORMS OR SIMILAR PRECEDENTS (i.e., PLEADINGS, MOTIONS, DEAL DOCUMENTS) THAT WILL HELP ME PREPARE THIS ASSIGNMENT?

When you are a Newbie Sister, you fear that this sort of question will make you seem like a lazy slug who is incapable of putting any original thought on paper. The opposite could not be more true. First, there's no reason to reinvent the wheel. Second, even if you have a pretty good idea as to how to draft something, oftentimes ASSes have their own format they like to use that captures their individual eccentricities and steers clear of their pet peeves.

Sidebar

For example, one of your authors incurred the wrath of a big-shot ASS when she used cross-references to define terms—a completely acceptable contract shorthand method. Instead, this ASS's pet peeve required her to repeat the text of the cross-reference *ad nauseum* throughout the document, thereby turning a 30-page document into a 50-page document. We can only guess that this ASS's client was paying by the page.

ARE THERE ANY SPECIFIC TOOLS AND/OR MATERIALS THAT YOU SUGGEST I START WITH TO RESEARCH THIS ARCANE ISSUE YOU DREAMED ABOUT IN THE MIDDLE OF YOUR VACATION?

If it's not obvious, don't be shy about getting the best resource list right from the horse's mouth. Those more experienced than yourself may have knowledge of the hidden treatise treasures and can point you in the right direction before you're unleashed to find the pirate's booty.

REPEAT THE ASSIGNMENT BACK TO THE ASS AND BE SURE TO ASK A LOT OF FOLLOW-UP QUESTIONS TO MAKE SURE THERE IS A MEETING OF THE MINDS. [39]

While lawyers are touted as the great communicators, when it comes to sitting in the ASS's office and receiving assignments on the low couch, we are so worried about how to act and appear intelligent that more times than not, the cat gets our tongues. You can't read the ASS's mind, so you must make every effort to understand exactly what he wants, even if it requires asking numerous follow-up questions.

Remember, there is no stupid question before you start to bill on a task. After you run up a $20,000 tab researching the wrong statute, however, every question you pose and almost everything you ask thereafter will seem quite dim-witted. Sometimes it helps to repeat the issue back to the ASS to see if they concur, but don't be surprised if, like a criminal defendant, they later change their story.

You will notice that almost invariably, all of the Top Brass' office chairs and couches are so low that guests sit at least one foot below even the most Napoleonic partner. Don't think for a minute that this is a coincidence.

*DECIDE IF YOU CAN REALISTICALLY GET THE ASSIGNMENT
DONE IN THE TIME FRAME GIVEN BASED
ON YOUR OTHER ASSIGNMENTS.*

It may take you a long time to learn this lesson, but it's an important one—assignments are like teenage sex, underage drinking, and illegal drugs—sometimes it's better to JUST SAY NO. As frightened as you may be of the ASSes, they would much prefer to have one assignment completed properly, than two done haphazardly. The best solution has always been that of honesty—you will need to communicate and tell them that you have two simultaneous deadlines. It's the partners' jobs to set the priorities, so let them duke it out.

Oftentimes, the multiple simultaneous deadlines are simply the result of, you guessed it, poor management. Attorneys have a very hard time managing their client's demands, so they promise them whatever it will take to make them happy at the expense of the health and happiness (what little there is left of that) of their **Sister** workhorses.

Once you've completed your assignment, you may be called into the ASS's office to discuss the project. Many times, you will be forced to sit on the low couch while the partner reads the entire memo—a painstaking and insufferable process. Inevitably, the partner will be interrupted by a call or two (typically personal) that lasts the better part of the hour. Every few minutes he may cover up the phone and whisper, *Hang on, this will only take another minute,* as you sink lower and lower into the low couch. As much as you'd like to file your nails and apply another coat of polish during his phone calls, you're better off just bringing other work into his office so that you can continue to bill while he's trying to schedule his tee time.

If you find yourself getting assignment after assignment from the same ASS, you may try to diversify yourself by asking other

ASSes if they need help with anything. You see, if you do a good job for one ASS, he may try to hoard you, because smart workaholic Newbies are a valuable commodity that ASSes don't like to share.

Legal Research Phobia

We've all been there, **Sisters**. The scenario goes something like this.

Big Muckety-Muck leaves a note on your chair that contains the following research assignment.

Does Client X's partnership qualify as a venture capital operating company so that its portfolio investment will be not be considered plan assets and therefore exempt from the rules and regulations promulgated under the Employee Retirement Income Security Act of 1974?

He also wants you to report back to him in one hour. You reread the note several thousand times until your apprehension manifests itself in a full-fledged case of the CRAPs—Chronic Research Anxiety Phobia Syndrome.

Never fear—ALL of us have had the CRAPs at some point in our career. Before wasting precious billables scanning the miles of library shelves looking for any book remotely related to the indiscernible assignment and aggravating your case of the CRAPs, there is a hierarchy of resources you may want to consult first.

SAINT GOOGLE (WWW.GOOGLE.COM)

If all of the words contained in the assignment sound like hieroglyphics, start with Saint Google, who will bless you with some sort of link to your ultimate goal so that you can get a clue.

COLLEAGUES IN YOUR GROUP

Even if the task seems so narrow and unprecedented that you are sure that you are the only one in the world who has even been asked to do it, you're probably wrong. Most associates have been there, done that, and can point you in the right direction.

TRADITIONAL LAW SCHOOL RESOURCES

If you know that your research assignment is limited to decisions in the southern district of Florida under Key West Number 283, you will be able to start with the basics you learned in law school.

LIBRARIANS

Librarians, if you're lucky enough to have them around, are your deities when it comes to research. They know the ins and outs of all of the materials out there, and chances are they've probably been asked about the area you're researching before.

800-WESTLAW-GODS (800-REF-ATTY)

This is a lawyer's best kept secret. You can actually call these reference people (oftentimes lawyers themselves who just didn't want to deal with the ASSes) and they will know the search engines that are appropriate for the information you are seeking and will oftentimes run the search for you at no charge.

Although research is time consuming and monotonous, from time to time you'll stumble upon authority for your client that will make your day, particularly when the facts of your case seem bleak and you feel like you are representing the wrong party. Consider this **Sister's** most remarkable victory.

> *I was representing a company being sued for sexual harassment whose indelicate male supervisor would greet all of his male co-workers with the phrase, "Now you're sucking cock." Much to my surprise, I found a series of cases (only in California, of course) holding that the mere exchange of profanity among men in the workplace does not create a hostile environment unless the victim believs the perpetrator wants the victim to perform said sexual act. What could be more entertaining than watching a government investigator ask twenty male coworkers if they actually believed that the supervisor wanted them to suck the former's cock?*

And who says legal research isn't fun.

Making Mistakes

As we mentioned earlier, the inevitable paradox about learning the ropes is that while the best way to learn is by trial and error, partners don't want to take the chance of having you make a mistake with their clients that could cost them business (and therefore their son's private school tuition).

— Sidebar —

A first-year Sister at a megafirm was given a two million dollar check from a senior partner to put in the client trust account late one evening. Since the administrator had left, she put the check into her pocket for safekeeping and went off with her colleagues for a nightcap at a local watering hole. After waking up with an excruciating hangover and limited memory of the previous evening's events, she picked up her jeans from the floor and discovered that the check was missing.

The reality, however, is that everyone makes mistakes and most of them are really meaningless—unless they actually result in harm to the client. In fact, we need to remind you that even highly-respected lawyers are committing much bigger and more egregious blunders than the grammar or punctuation boo-boos you recently committed.

— Sidebar —

Inquiring minds want to know what happened to the check and the Sister. The check vanished into thin air along with her memory of that night. However, this fun-loving, partying Sister is now a partner at the firm.

There is no mistake you cannot overcome if you handle the cleanup appropriately. Whatever you do, just make sure you've crafted a solution to your mistake (and calmed down) prior to running into the partner's office for confession.

Feedback, Anyone?

No matter how proactive partners are with their clients, they instantly become passive aggressive when it comes to their own staff. For some reason, while partners violently chew off the heads of their opponents, when it comes to conflict or giving bad news to one of their reports, they turn into big sissies. One Sister reported that she didn't receive a formal performance appraisal for over four years, and when she did, she was told no more than, *You're doing a good job.* In areas to improve, she was told she would *have to be more of an asshole if she wanted to make partner.* Not very helpful feedback by anyone's standards.

Not only should you *not* expect to receive substantive formal reviews, but you also shouldn't expect too much in the way of praise after performing first-class work. So how should you expect to get feedback in the practice of law? Generally, there are three pretty good indicators. First, you have the Red Sea. This is what your written product usually looks like after it has been marked up in red pen by an ASS. Although at first you will be mortified by the blood bath, it will actually serve as valuable information about how to improve your writing and research skills. Once in a while, you may even see a paltry *good argument* in the margin, although more often you are likely to see things like *AWK,*[40] *cite!*, or *WRONG.*

The second way you will know whether or not you pass muster is if the ASS gives you more work, because good work breeds more work (thus serving as an inducement for some of us to become dyslexic while working for the BBQ).

A third form of feedback, although less common than the first two, comes when you create such a work of art on an interesting topic that the partner tells you to turn it into an article. This piece of literary genius, written entirely by you, is then published in a prestigious law journal or state bar magazine under "Partner Name" (in big, bold print) "with help from Newbie Associate 𝕊𝕚𝕤𝕥𝕖𝕣" (in teensy-intsy smaller print).

In summary, there are a few things we hope you come away with when you battle the Beast within. First, those initial months (and even years) are filled with uncertainties about whether you are doing the right thing or more importantly, how to accomplish the right thing. For most of us, it's like freshman year of college—we feel totally out of control. Secondly, the more you think you know, the less you probably do know. It's only when you come to and are comfortable with the realization that there's always something else out there you need to learn or haven't discovered that you've truly grasped what it takes to be a *real lawyer*.

APPRECIATING THE QUEEN BEAST

Before you begin your journey into the world of law practice, you may truly believe *the firm* is one big happy family of lawyers, all of whom rake in oodles of money and share and share alike when they score a big client. Nothing could be further from the truth. In fact, the information about the inner mechanics of the firm (*i.e.*, their finances, operations, and politics) is typically guarded as closely as the gold at Fort Knox. It usually isn't until you've mortgaged your home to buy into the partnership that you learn the real scoop. While we can't tell you exactly how your employer functions, we can offer some insider information that will give you a behind-the-scenes glimpse of the Queen Beast.

Law Firm Economics 101

Don't be afraid to admit it—math and science just weren't your thing. Your shortfalls in these areas manifested as early as first grade, when you discovered you couldn't add or subtract any number greater than twenty (the total number of toes and fingers on your body). Science was no better to you. While all the other kids were dissecting pigs and frogs in seventh grade science lab, you were losing your lunch in the bathroom. So off you went to law school, where numbers were used for the exclusive purpose of calculating your GPA and science was only important for understanding how fast you could go into ketosis on the Atkins diet.

Nevertheless, if you want to comprehend the big picture about how your cog fits in the firm wheel, there is one simple formula you must process.

$$\text{REVENUES} - \text{EXPENSES} = \text{PROFIT}$$

Indulge us as we invoke classic statutory construction while we dissect each element of this formula.

REVENUES

This is the *moola* coming into the office. Where does this money come from? Clients. More specifically—the time and expenses you incur on behalf of clients. At most firms, the ultimate goal is to maximize revenue, which means servicing as many clients for as much of their work as possible.

EXPENSES

Expenses include, but are not limited to, the firm's rent (or mortgage), fancy furniture (like the low couches), high-priced artwork, equipment, supplies, extravagant firm lunches and parties, and last (but by no means least) your salary and benefits.

PROFIT

Profit is the money left over to compensate the owners of the firm (*i.e.*, the partners) after expenses are paid out of revenues. Speaking of partners' money, it's quite ironic that while the lockstep compensation paid to associates may as well be advertised on a billboard in Times Square, the amount of money that the partners pocket remains one of life's greatest mysteries to anyone outside the partner fraternity.

Manipulation of the Firm Formula

It's important to understand how the firm manipulates the formula and manages the economics of the firm. Following are some considerations that all firms face in this task.

ALLURING CLIENTS

With everyone and her **sister** getting a law degree, along with hundreds of megafirms sprouting up all over the country, even the big firms must vie for clients to stay in business.

As a result of this intense competition, all partners must shmooze to generate and keep business. This increased rivalry has resulted in a particularly bizarre practice called the *beauty contests*. A potential deep-pocket client is treated to over-the-top PowerPoint presentations and dog and pony shows by several different firms that promise to cure all of their company's ills on a shoestring budget. Thankfully, the contestants do not compete in a swimsuit or musical talent competition, but they still kiss enough proverbial ass to make the whole process seem ripe for Atlantic City.

The competition has become so fierce that the runner-ups have hired entire marketing departments to coach them to win the next pageant. These coaches not only work on the firm's website, brochures, public relations, and the like to get the word out that their law firm is the fairest of them all, they also put the presenters through a transformation akin to the television show *Queer Eye for the Straight Guy*.[41]

So what, you may ask, should you be doing to generate business? The answer for Newbies is usually *nothing*, but some firms will allocate a small budget (*i.e.*, think lunch at Hoolihans rather than The Ritz) to wine and dine potential clients. You will find

Oh, and did we happen to mention the perks of having your own clients? One Sister struck up such a close relationship with her high-end fashion client that she made her a custom gown for achieving such a great result in a litigation matter. If she didn't bring in the client, you can bet that gown would be hanging in someone else's closet.

that once you can bring in clients, the world is your oyster.

If you develop new business, not only will your bosses love you, oh holy revenue generator, but you can call the shots with your own clients. Additionally, this may alleviate your chances of getting stuck slaving away for the BBQ's clients.

APPEASING CLIENTS

Once the client is in the door, you have to understand that most partners will do nothing short of walking on water to make the client happy. If a client asks your boutique, intellectual property firm if it can litigate a white collar crime, guess who represents that *Of course my firm can do it,* and then hires a third-party firm for consultation but requests that you become an overnight expert in the field?

Perhaps someday partners will learn to manage their clients in a more appropriate fashion, but until that day comes, partners will remain slaves to their clients just as much as you are a slave to the partners. In any event, at the end of the day, a firm is worth nothing more than the services it offers. Remember—the only thing that promotes a firm's services (besides the ill-fated beauty contests) is the firm's reputation. A good reputation (*i.e.,* meeting every demand of crazy clients) generates more clients and billables, while a bad one will send the firm into extinction.

SHOW ME THE MONEY!

Once you represent the client and have billed what feels like a lifetime to its client ID number, only half the revenue battle is won. Why? Because not everything that is billed is collected. First, there is a chance that the billing partner will dock your hours if he thinks that billing twenty hours for shepardizing a case, for example, is just a tad bit excessive.

As an aside, we note that as a Newbie associate, you will generally always think that you have taken too long to complete a project. It's not your responsibility to report fewer hours than those that you actually worked, even if you think something took you too long to accomplish.

However, all *docking* should take place by the partner and the partner alone (although it's more likely that the partner will *enhance* rather than *dock* if he feels you were a bit too expedient on the matter).

The second, and more likely scenario, is that of the deadbeat client who doesn't pay the firm's bills. The *collections* part of the revenue equation is actually a more important number than the number of billables generated. Oftentimes, if the client continues to ignore a firm's bills despite numerous threatening letters, the firm winds up writing off the balance at the end of the year rather than sending Tony Soprano out to collect. Of course, writing off charges can turn into an insurmountable problem when a firm relies on one client for the majority of its revenues and moneybags client refuses to pay, or worse yet, files for bankruptcy.

THE DELICATE BALANCE BETWEEN EXPENSES AND PROFITS

While everyone at the firm agrees that maximizing revenues is a good thing, there are competing goals when it comes to attributing the revenues to either the expense or profit side of the equation. In other words, the more the commoners (*i.e.*, nonpartners) take home, the less the greedy partners can take and vice versa. It's a perpetual tug-of-war. Thus, you will need to earn your keep in order to justify a partner's relinquishing of his precious profits to pay your salary. For this reason, many firms will institute certain ratios that validate your existence in their legal world. A typical revenue to expense ratio in many firms is 4:1—that is, your billing should bring revenues into the firm that are four times as much as the firm pays you in salary. Keep in mind that the greedy partners do not necessarily take home the other 75% of the revenues—at least half of it goes to paying other overhead and expenses, and the *little* that is left over will go towards paying for the partners' villas in Tuscany and their fancy cars.

And while we're giving away the bank, we have another insider doozy for you. At most of the lockstep firms, your billing rate corresponds with your years of tenure at the firm, which increases with each anniversary you are at the firm (usually this falls in September). However, at most firms, the salary increase associated with your class year billing rate does not occur until January. Therefore, many firms will collect a premium on your experience for three months even if you are not paid accordingly.

Even if a firm is kind with associate salaries, such generosity may come at a big price. Take, for example, the case of Brobeck, Phleger & Harrison, LLP, a once techie-firm in northern California. During the Internet bubble, Brobeck partners were living large and took the dramatic move of increasing first year salaries up to $125,000, hoping to lure all the Harvard brainiacs out west. The rest is history. Brobeck's attempt to outsmart the market backfired, and all those hot-shot lawyers were left unemployed as the oh-so-generous firm filed for bankruptcy. A heartrendering [42] demise, indeed.

DOWN TIMES

Unlike Brobeck, however, most firms have a plan in place for managing the slow times. As much as we cry poverty because the lockstep salary system stymies huge financial growth, it does have a built-in insurance policy. During financial downtimes at a firm (*i.e.*, no work or abysmal collection rates), revenues are driven down while you continue to earn your lockstep compensation, which results in partners tightening their belts, not the associates. Not bad for a union member, eh?

In downtimes, most firms will make every effort to cut nonassociate related expenses (think no more fancy lunches or Pilot pens) to salvage your salary and job. During the really bad times, some firms will have no choice but to lay off associates. Before you get all bent out of shape, however, you should remember that associate layoffs are extremely rare.

At many firms, one would need to do nothing short of snorting crack on a partner's desk to get fired (assuming the partner was not an eager participant). Even if you are very slow (*i.e.*, billing more hours to reading romance novels than client work), layoffs are rare because it's typically part of a cycle and business usually picks up at some point. The costs associated with laying off an associate, followed by recruiting and training a new associate (not to mention paying off a headhunter who gets a sweet ⅓ of the incoming associate's salary) far exceeds the revenue loss associated with your becoming an authority on Jackie Collins.

FIRM POLITICS

Some of the most profitable firms in history have disbanded simply due to ego incompatibility (*i.e.*, partners who were never taught by their mommies to respect others and share with their friends in the sandbox).

Although partners will generally try to keep the behind-the-scenes soap opera under raps, someone usually leaks to his or her *trusted associate* who will, in turn, spread the news to the rest of the kids. If you scrape beneath the surface, you will actually discover that at most firms, there are factions of partners who group together to protect their fiefdoms like the Montagues and Capulets. Apparently, selecting the proper alliance is critical to long-term survival in the partnership. The kiddie associates, like offspring of divorced parents, are placed in the sole custody of one parent.

We are also told that in some extreme cases, there are factions of partners that are such bitter rivals that they won't even speak to each other, share associates or work product, and may even compete for the same clients. They are placed on different floors of the firm and enter into temporary restraining order-like agreements that they will stay away from each other's associates and current clients. If the relationship goes south, the parties will go to an informal mediation to resolve any disputes.

Why does the firm tolerate such childlike behavior? You guessed it—money. If each of the warring factions has a substantial client base, the firm would rather host the Cold War than lose those precious revenues. If the sandbox still isn't big enough under this arrangement, a divorce is inevitable and the entire firm may disband, no matter how profitable the entity is, and dissolution results in a lot of unemployed kiddies.

Firm Morale

The third key to comprehension of the Queen Beast is getting a feel for the firm morale and culture. In short, some contend that it's better to work at a financially challenged, disorganized firm that is home to happy associates than to toil away at the billion-dollar Warren Buffet-run firm home to utter misery.

Let's face it—you have enough stress on your plate with learning the ropes and satisfying crazy client needs. The last thing you need is a bunch of kiss-ass, gunner, cutthroat rivals or partners who haze for the fun of it. In any event, an unhappy group of associates can also result in a mass exodus, leaving you the last associate standing to do the grunt work (although it is more likely you will go with them if it gets that bad).

Enough about business. Onto socializing the Beast....

SOCIALIZING THE BEAST

If you didn't glaze over and fall into a drooling stupor while reading the last section, you probably came away wondering, *Why would greedy partners dole out the dough for social events that decrease the firm's profits, whereby leaving less money in their own pockets?* We think the answer is fourfold.

We note that the range of social functions will, of course, depend on the size of the firm (the bigger the better), the area of the country (the more urban, the better) and the firm's culture (the more flamboyant, the better). Therefore, much of the material contained in this section will only apply to Sisters practicing at large firms in a big city.

First, firms need to impress potential recruits and clients. Second, as intelligent as we lawyers are (and, admittedly, cocky), we have a low tolerance for boredom. Third, expenses associated with entertaining are, ironically, classified as *reasonable and necessary* under the tax code (although they are usually neither), and therefore, the firm generally receives a tax deduction for incurring such expenses. Fourth, and perhaps most significantly, it is the firm's temporary solution to the eternal associate complaint, *I have no life.*

The Events

So, how will your employer provide you with a *life*? While the events will run the gamut, you can be sure of one overriding theme attributable to all employer-hosted events—food, food, oh, that glorious food. Many Sisters confess that eating at the top places in town and gorging at events catered by world-renowned chefs is *the* highlight of practicing law.

Consider Tim and Nina Zagat, who built an empire from their love of food. The infamous founders of the Zagat's guide were, you guessed it, both lawyers billing away at big law firms in NYC. They launched the first Zagat survey in 1979 as a hobby to keep track of all of the fabulous gastronomic choices available in Manhattan. Believe us when we tell you that you are about twenty times more likely to find the burgundy bible in any Sister's credenza than to find the Bluebook of Citations.

THE SUMMER ASSOCIATE AND RECRUITING BOONDOOGLE

The *Summer Associate Delusion* (SAD) program will allow you to wine and dine the poor young saps with all sorts of extravaganzas, all while the only Shuga Daddy some of us will ever know (the firm) foots the bill. As an associate, you are now in the driver's seat for making plans, and if you buddy up to the summer associate coordinator (or better yet, get on the summer associate committee), you can get permission to partake in any activity you just don't want to pay for yourself. Want to take a dinner-cruise around the city? Tickets to *Cirque du Soleil*? Urban rock climbing? Box seats to a coveted baseball game? White water rafting? Cooking class? Wine tasting? We'll stop before we get carried away [43], but the point is that it's all there for the taking, so long as you drag a summer associate along with you.

The Holiday Party

While the firm's holiday party is typically the high point for staff (who will incessantly remind you that they are never wined and dined), it is the low-point for most attorneys who would rather spend their nonbillable time on the couch with a pint of Chubby Hubby than making nice with the partners and staff. On the day of the party, expect next to no services, because most secretaries will invariably spend the majority of the day primping in the bathroom until they've finished every last ounce of that nasty can of hairspray. Not unlike a porn movie, expect to see nothing less than all the sequins, miniskirts, neon makeup, big hair, and cleavage that you can imagine—and then some. With alcohol flowing freely and mistletoes strategically placed everywhere, hookups are inevitable—which provide enough gossip fodder for the entire firm until the next holiday party. Perhaps this would explain why spouses are NEVER invited to these shindigs.

The Summer Party

Some firms will also host a summer party, which is usually held on a weekday so you get to miss an entire day of work. Of course, you'd probably rather spend the day at *Neiman Marcus* and the spa, but most firms require your attendance. Somehow the term *mandatory party* seems a bit absurd, but you really can't complain about a day in the sun instead of the florescent lights. Many of these parties are held at one of the partner's stodgy country clubs, so not only must you wake up extra early (to meet for the dreaded 7 a.m. tee-times) but you also have to wear those godforsaken whites that make you look five pounds heavier all day long. If you are unfortunate enough not to come from the Rockefeller family,

Sidebar

So, what is proper pool attire? You will probably obsess and debate this issue for hours on end with your Sisters prior to the big day. While most choose to cover up and sweat to death, some will actually whip out the bathing suit and even more egregious, the sexy thong bikini. Trust us, anything short of Taliban style cabana wear around the pool at a firm party will get you remembered for all the wrong reasons, even if you have a hot bod.

chances are you may not even play golf or tennis, so you will have no choice but to sit around the pool all day long until cocktails and dinner are served.

Happy Hours

Many firms will host Friday night happy hours to celebrate the end of the work week and the beginning of the (working) weekend. While Newbie associates relish winding down over greasy finger food and booze, they will soon figure out that there is no such thing as a free Hiney and piggy-in-a-blanket.

First, if you stay for happy hour, you will invariably work later than if you opt for the Friday night bolt-out-the-door-early escape. The extra hours that are billed on account of waiting for the happy hour more than pay for the chicken sate skewers. Second, and even more dangerous, is the risk that you will get snagged for weekend work when you were not planning to be there. The partners and Bubble Associates know that if you're not swamped enough to forego happy hour, you must be *light*. You will know you're screwed when a senior associate approaches you by the sushi tray and asks, *You busy?* Or says, *I hear you have some time.* For this reason, it is not uncommon to see associates (who have learned their lesson the hard way) sneak into the happy hour, swipe two beers and a plate full of sushi rolls, and bolt out the door.

On the upside, however, attending the cocktail parties gives you the opportunity to hobnob with lawyers working in other departments. And if you are single, you may discover that your Prince Charming is only a few floors away.

Birthday Parties

Let's face it—everyone wants to feel like a queen on her birthday. Just know that it's nearly impossible to be productive, because you spend the day:

- talking to people who stop by your office to wish you a happy birthday;
- going on extended lunches with your Bingin' and Bitchin' Buddies; and,
- fielding calls (and hopefully large flower deliveries) from friends and family.

Nevertheless, the firm may guilt you into doing some work on your big day because they will throw you the infamous office birthday party. The routine is always the same. You are lured into a conference room under some lame pretense. Thankfully, though, this is the one day of the year that your heart won't sink in fear of being stuck on an all-night emergency project, because you know what's coming. When you enter the room, everyone sings Happy Birthday—out of tune—and you continue the charade by acting surprised and grateful. As soon as the last note is hit, all the lawyers make a run for the door with cake in hand. After sugaring you up, you will probably return to your desk and feel guilted into billing a few hours to thank the firm for their ostensible thoughtfulness.

Everyday Life

As you will soon find out, although we are all grown-ups by the time we begin working at the firm, our behavior at the office oftentimes is no different than the way it was in high school. We relish in the gossip about who is dating whom; we eat in a cafeteria (at some big firms); we keep an extra set of gym clothes in our *lockers* (desk drawers); and, as each year passes, we get more and more excited about looking at the pictures of the new class of incoming associates in the firm's pig book.

Most **Sisters** report that many years after they leave the sweatshop, they remain the best of friends with the associates that were hazed along with them. The irony is, while most associates embrace their social lives within the firm (mostly because they don't have time to keep one outside the firm), many report that the partners remain oddly remote. From avoiding eye contact in the bathrooms and elevators to communicating solely by email, you would think that some of the partners were fugitives, rather than practitioners of the law.

Weekending at the Firm

One last unplanned social activity that is worth noting is *weekending at the firm*. No, it is not the Hamptons or Vegas, but the office can be very amusing if you have to drag your butt there on one of your precious Saturdays or Sundays. The good news about working all weekend is that clothes (and hygiene, unfortunately) don't matter. Because the phones aren't ringing much and the weekend secretarial temps usually don't take as many ciggie breaks as your normal secretary, you can generally work much more efficiently than on a weekday. Ironically, you will find that as pissed off as you are that you have to be there all weekend, you will spend almost as much time complaining about the fact that you are there with your other work-plagued Sisters than you do actually billing.

The free food is also a plus. A typical Saturday may start with your picking at the left-over donuts in the conference room before turning on your computer. By 11 a.m., you've collected all of your take-out menus, read the latest restaurant reviews, and started calling around to see who's around to partake in the lunch binge with you. Once all the weekenders agree on their order (which typically takes no less than one hour to coordinate), you anxiously wait for the delivery in the lobby. Nothing short of a two-hour lunch will do on a weekend. Leisurely consuming the goodies in a conference room, the weekenders will partake in long, drawn out conversations about anything not having to do with work.

As much as you promise yourself that you will go home for dinner, by 6 p.m. you realize that you just procrastinated the whole bloody day away. Before you know it, you find yourself stuck at the firm through the late evening, during which you take breaks from your work with the other weekenders by going shopping in the supply cabinet *gift shop* for your special Pilot pens, sending joke voicemail messages from partners' phones to unsuspecting Affable Alligators, and searching for unguarded candy dishes. Right before you're ready to depart, you go online to buy tickets for the midnight movies. And who says lawyers don't know how to have fun?

BEAUTY AND THE BEAST

What should you take away from our discussion of the Beast? The practice of law involves much more than simply research and writing—it's about learning how to satisfy unreasonable client and partner demands; understanding how the firm operates and makes money; and lastly, but perhaps most significantly, maintaining your sanity by leaning on friends at the firm who will help you through the bittersweet times. But most of all, don't let the ASSes give you CRAP—you're just as smart as they are. You just need time to become as quirky and eccentric as your new subculture. Then you, too, will become an ASS!

■ ■ ■

10

Fighting for the Perfect Pair of Shoes

-litigators-

ave you ever fought over a pair of shoes at a sample sale? Do you get a charge out of battling for a parking spot or preventing other drivers from cutting you off? Does winning an argument over minutia with your significant other get you all riled up? If your answer is yes to any of these questions, you may have the stomach for litigation.

Make no mistake—litigation may transform you into a true shark (and we mean that only as the highest compliment). Even if you manage to litigate gracefully, we guarantee that you will run up against a barracuda or two sometime in your career. But don't fret, **Sister**, we'll help you navigate through the unchartered waters with style and grace.

SISTERS' SECRET WEAPONS

As a general matter, neophyte **Sister** litigators bide most of their time researching and writing esoteric legal issues and have very little, if any, exposure to case management. However, we would suggest that if you understand the strategies frequently employed by litigators, you will have a better understanding of how your cog fits in the wheel, thereby making the grunt work in your young and tender years a little more meaningful. Taking a cue from the Y-Factor Sports Gene, we have created the Sisters' *Playbook of Winning Moves*, which highlights the strategic plays commonly employed by fellow litigators. Following each move is a suggested *counterattack* that we have found most befitting.

Play #1: Scorch the Earth Litigation

Not favored or encouraged, *scorch the earth litigation* is the equivalent of holding up a bank. Usually, one side will prepare a complaint by throwing every cause of action imaginable against the wall and seeing what will stick. We're talking a claim for *buggery* (the refined British word for naughty sex) in a shareholder's derivative suit. Even if the lawsuit is a slam dunk loser, the other side banks on the fact that it will cost your client *beaucoup* bucks to dismiss all of the bogus claims. While at first glance it will appear that the house is favored to win (as your client cries mercy and begs to settle), a fierce counterattack can turn the tables.

Counterattack #1: If your client is loaded and wants retribution, the best tactic is to get the lawsuit dismissed and seek attorneys' fees and costs as sanctions against the lawyer and/or the client for filing the frivolous (a legalese favorite for groundless) lawsuit. If your client can't afford to fight, then the mission is to try and settle for *bubkus* (our favorite Yiddish word for *very little*). In some cases, you may be able to play the *BK Card* (bankruptcy, not Burger King) by threatening to file bankruptcy on behalf of your client, leaving the plaintiff with a judgment worth nothing more than the paper it is written on.

Play #2: *Hasta La Vista* Litigation

In this play, your opposing counsel thinks he is Aah-nowd Schwarzenegger (that's the actor, not the governor) in *Terminator*. With his deadly weapon (Microsoft Word), he writes hateful and intolerable accusatory letters personalizing the dispute as if you committed the wrong yourself. Every day of the case you will pray that the terminator, his despicable client, and the dispute will vanish into thin air—*Hasta la vista, baby*. Unwilling to even acknowledge that your client has a position, any communication from you just adds fuel to the fire.

Counterattack #2: The only way to resolve a case driven by an overly zealous attorney is to win it—either by motion or at trial. Letters and civil conversations will not cut it. Occasionally, a third party can hammer some sense into the terminator's head, but don't count on it. Put on your bulletproof vest and prepare for trial.

Play #3: *It's Not Fair* Litigation

Remember when you were grounded as a child and sent to your room for stealing your kid sibling's stuff? Since you didn't have a leg to stand on, the best you could muster was a whiney—*It's not fair* —and hope for some clemency. It rarely worked as a child and it's even less likely to persuade anyone when uttered by an adult. Yet we see it all the time—a party bases an entire lawsuit on the mistaken belief that certain conduct is unfair and therefore (in their *legal expertise*—worth *bubkus*), unlawful. Dealing with your opposition is like potty training a child—lots of handholding, lack of control, and (unlike potty training) no matter what you say or do, they never get it.

Counterattack #3: Take a Valium (figuratively speaking, of course) to calm your nerves, because no matter how many times you explain the obvious, your opposition will require you to jump through every hoop. Our advice—act like your mother—at first nurturing, then nagging, and finally threatening. If they refuse to dismiss or settle for a nominal amount, employ Counterattack #1.

Play #4: White Shoe Litigation

White Shoe litigation does exist, although some would say it's a dying art. All counsel are pleasant—even friendly—with each other and respect the other sides' differing positions. Requests and favors are always granted and time frames are always extended indefinitely. No hate mail or threats are ever exchanged. After both sides have built up their cases, they seek resolution amicably or try the case.

Counterattack #4: Savor the moment! This is the idyllic scenario that your law professors (who never practiced law or can no longer remember how to litigate) described. Whatever you do, though, don't mistake the lack of correspondence or civility for laziness or ineptitude.

THE DISCOVERY DIET

Don't be fooled by the term *discovery*, **Sisters**. It is an oxymoron as used in the practice of law, because the object of the game is to manipulate and limit the information that gets discovered by the other side (although you will try to extract everything you need for your case). Let us guide you through the discovery process—**Sister** style.

Heaping Servings of Written Discovery

Litigators diet on large portions of written discovery, which is the equivalent of fat-free rice cakes (tasteless, but good for you). From the second a lawsuit is filed, we recommend that you send over a heaping serving of discovery requests (seeking information from the other party) and deposition notices.

It's no different from a sample sale. First in line gets priority. And whatever you do, make sure you ask for everything under the sun, even if it's only remotely relevant. Mom was right when she told you—*If you don't ask, you won't get.*

When responding to the opposing party's discovery requests (seeking information from your client), the name of the game is volume over substance. File lengthy objections killing as many trees as possible, then, notwithstanding the objections, either agree to surrender or withhold the information. Initially, you may want to be aggressive and withhold information in order to feel out whether your opposition is sleeping, lazy, or too overworked to take you to court to obtain the information. If you play hard-ball, you hold your breath waiting to see if the other side brings a timely Motion to Compel you to produce the information. If your opposition blows the deadline, your dirty little secrets stay with you and your client and you don't have to turn the requested items over before trial. If, however, your opposition files a Motion to Compel (and you can bet a motion seeking sanctions against you for unjustifiably withholding the information), you either turn it over at that point or duke it out in court.

And you thought Judge Judy was exciting.

Snooping in the Third Party Pantry for Other Goodies

Seasoned Sisters all agree that the truth is rarely told 100% of the time (or anywhere close). Your job is to uncover all of the untruths and misrepresentations made by the other side (and in many cases, your own client). *Third party subpoenas* are cheap and highly effective tools to do just that. Medical records and divorce files containing juicy admissions are the perfect recipes to toast and burn your opposition's case. At the very least, it allows you to bill for reading Harlequinesque sagas.

The Deposition Recipe, Sister Style

Most Sisters agree the only day that they don't obsess over fat and food is D-Day (deposition day, not donut day). The fact of the matter is that you can't interrogate and stuff your face at the same time. On D-Day, pretend you are Katie Couric—not because she has shapely legs and wears great shoes (although come to think of it, that too), but because everyone loves her and wants to open up to her, even if they disagree with her views.

Let's start with the basics, ladies. A deposition is not just an excuse to bill eleven hours in a day and stare out the conference room window. It is a proceeding that is conducted outside of the courtroom where one party asks another person questions about the case under oath. The information obtained (or not obtained, as the case may be) is critical, as this testimony has the same force and effect as if the person was testifying in a court of law.

Deposition day can be nerve-racking to even the most experienced. Although there are oodles of preparation techniques and deposition styles, we provide you here with a list (in no particular order) of the top 10 tips that Sisters far and wide recommend for taking and defending depositions.

VIDEOGRAPHER AND INTERPRETER SERVICES

Consider videotaping the deposition—costly, yes, but highly effective when a deponent adjusts her bra strap every time she lies. Also, consider hiring an interpreter. Expensive, time-consuming, and confusing to the parties, but necessary if the deponent doesn't speak a word of English or conveniently claims he does not *comprende* your questions on the day of deposition (despite the fact that he had a twenty-minute conversation in English about the Yankees' stats with the hot dog guy under the umbrella during break).

HONE UP ON INTERROGATION TECHNIQUES

Simulate your parents' obsessive line of questioning during your adolescent years—who, what, where, when, how are mandatory questions, and then obtain supporting documents. If you blocked out your earlier years (with or without the help of therapy), treat it no differently than conducting due diligence on a first date.

DISCREDIT ADVERSE DEPONENTS

When a nonparty witness gives damaging testimony, your job is to establish that the party, lawyers, and witnesses are all in bed together (literally and figuratively, depending on the case). Ask them to describe their relationship and then probe into everything they have ever done together, including sharing a scone before the deposition began. Of course, there is nothing better than finding out the deponent is *shagging* (another refined British word for...well, you know) one of the opposing parties.

HIRE A FAVORABLE COURT REPORTER

Not only will he or she give you an objective assessment of the testimony, if he or she is *your court reporter* (*i.e.*, the one you hire for every deposition you take), you may also benefit from valuable confidences overheard in the hallway or bathroom. Also, when everyone in the room starts talking over each other, which inevitably happens, you can bet the written transcript stands a better chance of appearing more favorable to your client.

PLAY THE GOOD COP

Play the Good Cop all the way to the end, **Sister**. You have only one shot at a deponent, so make him or her feel all warm and fuzzy inside while simultaneously snatching the info you need.

DON'T FORGET THE GOODY BAGS

Always ask for any documents you subpoenaed at the outset, because the deponent may have brought you a goody bag far superior to any favors received at kiddie birthday parties.

CLOSE THE DOOR

Remember how your mother used to nag you to close the door on cold days? Always ask,

> *"Is there anything else you haven't told me about ___?"*

To prevent being blindsided, keep prodding away to see if you can help jog the deponent's memory, using questions such as, *"Are there any documents that will help you remember ___ ?"*

GET THE GOSSIP

Second- or third-hand information is fair game on D-Day—your friend *hearsay* is welcome at this party. Don't forget to ask about what rumors may be circulating around town. Chances are, there may be some truth to them.

BREAKS

Eavesdropping in the hallway, deposition room, bathroom, or any other public place is fair play.

One Sister went to the bathroom to *powder her nose.* As she was applying the proverbial powder, she heard the expert deponent and opposing counsel talking to each other between bathroom stalls. The Sister heard the expert tell the lawyer about the holes in her case, while the opposing counsel responded that she just wanted to settle. Lesson learned? Nothing's sacred in the bathroom—even among women.

DEFENDING DEPOSITIONS

When your client is in the hot seat, your goal in defending the deposition is to get it over with quickly without giving the other side any ammunition. One of our favorite defensive deposition techniques was employed by one smooth-talking silver-haired gentleman (who incidentally served as the leader of the free world for eight years) when he was questioned about certain marital infidelities. After each and every question posed, this southern gentleman asked the meaning of each and every word in the question, including what exactly was meant by the word *is*. More than once the interrogating attorney cried mercy and simply abandoned certain lines of questioning. While the rest of the country was criticizing this unnamed poor soul from Arkansas, litigators commended him for a job well done.

If phrased the right way, your objections will not only disrupt the questioner, but will also give your client hints on how to answer the questions.

Sister Litigators' Dietary Supplements

Litigators supplement their diet by employing teams of essential accessories—spies, experts, and consultants—to help them gather information to bolster their clients' positions.

UNDERCOVER INVESTIGATORS

On certain types of matters, working up the case often requires you to test the credibility of the key players and the authenticity of the evidence. Because the events in dispute are rarely proven by direct evidence, the only way to test the weight of circumstantial evidence is to hire a private investigator—your spy on a payroll. Sisters don't ask how they obtain the information—you just don't want to know.

CONSULTANTS AND EXPERTS

Sisters often hire consultants to help them work up a case. The consultants are covered by the attorney-client privilege and therefore, any communications with them cannot be revealed to the other side.

One Sister told us of defending an elderly client who swore that he had no idea who wrote a very damaging document. The client testified in a deposition that it was not his handwriting, but his testimony just didn't pass the *smell test* (a lawyer phrase for I think he's lying). So, she hired her own handwriting consultant, who confirmed (with a 99% probability) that it was in fact the client's handwriting. This little fib not only exposed the client to civil liability, but also criminal prosecution for perjury. Talk about biting the hand that feeds you!

Experts, on the other hand, are not protected by the attorney-client privilege, so theoretically all communications between you (or your opposing counsel) and an expert may be discoverable. Experts are usually allowed to testify when the subject matter is not understandable to the jurors. We don't mean to be condescending (even though it's one of those nasty traits that automatically comes along with membership to the Sisterhood), but since most jurors seem to have flunked out of phonics, this standard is almost always met.

Once qualified, the expert is retained to *objectively* consider the evidence. Like everything else in life, there is nothing objective about the expert or the process. We have yet to meet an expert who has testified against a client who was paying their $500 per hour bill.

TAKING YOUR ACT ON THE ROAD

At some point in time, all litigators must take their act on the road and actually argue their clients' position to a judge, jury, mediator, arbitrator, administrative officer, or other decision-maker.

King of the Hill: The Court Clerk

While the judge and law clerk may rule the law, the Court Clerk rules the courtroom. Plant your lips on his or her behind, because if you misbehave, you can be sure the entire courthouse personnel will hear about it by lunchtime. If you play your cards right, the Court Clerk may also give you the unwritten rules of the courtroom.

Consider Trial's Kinder Cousin: Mediation and Arbitration

These days, you may want to consider resolving your clients' disputes in an *alternative dispute resolution* (ADR) forum rather than going to trial. Basically, all litigators have the same wish when they blow out their birthday candles—for their clients to pay their bills and resolve all disputes outside of the courtroom. Why? Because there are no winners at trial and ADR is usually faster and cheaper.

Mediations and arbitrations are usually conducted behind closed doors. Therefore, the success or failure of the process will oftentimes depend on the choice of the mediator or arbitrator. So, whatever you do, research your choice carefully and make sure you pick the best person to resolve the particular dispute (in your client's favor, of course). Consider the individual's experience, methods, problem-solving skills, people skills, perseverance, persuasiveness, and in the case of a mediator, the likeliness he or she will strong-arm the parties to compromise and settle the matter.

Sidebar

Mediation occurs when an independent person (the mediator) informally shuttles between the parties in an effort to resolve the dispute. Prior to the mediation, the parties submit briefs setting forth their positions. At the mediation, the mediator beats each party into submission by exposing the holes in their case and the costs—emotionally and financially—if the case does not settle.

Arbitration is where an independent third party (arbitrator) serves as the judge and jury in the case, with typically relaxed rules of evidence. If the arbitration is binding, the arbitrator's decision is final (with a few limited exceptions that are rarely met).

T – R – I – A – L

If there was a reality television show depicting trial lawyers, no one would become a litigator. After months of writing nasty-grams, drafting hateful motions, and wrestling with the discovery beast, you must wait for a firm trial date, which can take months or even years. Once the trial finally begins, the pressure and time commitment triples. Not only must you present your case expediently, preserve evidentiary objections, and successfully poke holes in the other side's case, you must also contend with the arbitrary decision-making of the judge and jury, your uncontrollable witnesses, and let us not forget, your agitated client. One mistake at trial can cost your client his or her life or significant monetary damages (which in some client's opinions, is worth more than their lives).

And then, let us not forget the anticlimactic nature of it all as we recount one **Sister's** tale about her first civil trial experience.

Although I had prepared for trial hundreds of times, this time it was different because there would be no surrender—both sides were planted in their positions and the stakes were too high. Afraid of screwing up, I prepared my witnesses for hours on end until they recited their lines flawlessly. While each moment of my first trial was as tense and nerve racking as each point at a Wimbledon final, nothing was as invigorating as the final moments of the trial when the decision was rendered in my client's favor.

Empowered by my first victory, I felt like a school kid running home to my parents to tell them the good news. Unlike my parents' responses to my academic milestones, the victory was not as well received by my client. In fact, his response can best be summed up by the verbatim words that he used: "What did all this bull**** cost me? For the cost of your f—ckin' services defending against this scumbag's frivolous case, I could've bought ...." Needless to say, our bill was negotiated for months after the trial and ultimately the client was rushed to the hospital with severe chest pain after he received the Notice of Appeal.

This is why most cases settle, **Sister**.

OUR CLOSING STATEMENTS

Thanks to litigators, we are no longer driving SUV's with exploding tires or taking Fen-Phen to shed weight. Unfortunately, however, the cost of achieving justice is far outweighed by the cost of settling quietly. If litigation is your calling, you will need to become accustomed to playing ball on an uneven field with Vegas-like odds. You will win some motions and cases you should lose, and you will lose some you should win.

We're not saying that the system is completely arbitrary, but sometimes no matter how hard you prepare and how *right* your client is, it won't always go your way. Because it is a costly gamble to place important disputes in the hands of judges and juries, you will need to develop creative, cost-efficient solutions. If you can live with these odds and you can stomach the contentiousness of it all (and have the patience to do a lot of research and writing in your early years of practice) you will find it quite rewarding. If not, the **Sisterhood** still welcomes you to the world of *transactional law*.

■ ■ ■

11

Persuasively Negotiating a Shoe Purchase

-transactional lawyers-

h ow does a **Sister** decide that corporate law may be her calling? Consider the following true tale.

*Once upon a time, there was a smart little girl who knew she wanted to be a
lawyer as early as grammar school when she watched "To Kill a Mockingbird."
In high school and college, she and her friends had weekly "The Practice" parties. She even idolized "Ally McBeal" (even though she thought Ally should eat
a cookie now and then). And forget trying to get a date with her on "Law and
Order" or "Judging Amy" night.*

*When she entered law school, she was surprised to learn that the draconian
procedural rules of evidence annoyed her and the unscripted public speaking in
Trial Procedure class made her anxious, while Contracts and Property classes,
on the other hand, were a breeze. Nevertheless, after law school, it was off to
the big litigation firm where she planned to become a powerful courtroom
attorney. Instead, she spent long and painfully boring days researching and
writing memorandum, coding documents, and drafting perfunctory motions.*

*After six months of this agony, she wanted to toss her hands up and say
enough with this crap and go fold sweaters at the GAP. Unfortunately, her
mean Aunt Sallie Mae said—No Way. She knew she would have to find some*

way out of this predicament. Luckily, her firm had a departmental rotation system, and she chose to get away from the litigation drudgery by buying some time with the transactional attorneys before deciding what she wanted to be when she grew up. As it turned out, she had the flair for detail needed to draft difficult contracts, and a personality perfectly suited to reaching agreements upon, rather than winning, issues presented. She lived happily ever after in a practice area that better suited her personality and style.

THE DECISION

Many Sisters find themselves in the boardroom rather than the courtroom by default. You see, the problem with choosing a career in corporate law is that the general public equates law with litigation. Law school contributes to this problem by predominantly teaching the case study method. Cases arise from litigation, so even corporate transactions tend to be taught by reading about disputes arising from breach of contract or securities matters that have resulted in litigation. Thus, most lawyers graduate from law school not even giving a thought to becoming a corporate lawyer. And because many Sisters despise anything having to do with numbers, accounting, or economics, they believe the courtroom will shield them from the quantitative drudgery.

Hollywood doesn't do much to glamorize transactional law either. After all, we have yet to see a movie or television show starring dozens of attorneys, accountants, actuaries, and investment bankers doing nothing but slaving over football fields full of boxes conducting due diligence and then negotiating over sentence structure, with the climax of the show being the fistfight over the comma placement at the printers.

Nevertheless, many find transactional work more tolerable and satisfying than they ever imagined. Fighting is not a prerequisite of the job and there is a high probability of a *win-win* outcome—something that is rare, if not impossible, in litigation. You should also know that even if you were an accounting drop out and haven't taken any math courses since high school, you really don't have to be an Adam Smith to be a great corporate lawyer.

Many also mistakenly believe that transactional law is *man's work*. However, if you buy into all of the *Mars/Venus* hype, some say that Sisters are actually genetically wired to be great negotiators. While the Y-Factor gets off on nothing short of victory, we women tend to focus on communicating (big surprise, right?), building consensus, encouraging openness, tolerating differences, and identifying problems quickly and accurately.[44] We are also known to be better listeners (after years of dating, we should think so) and in negotiations it is critical to hear out the other side out and identify the hidden messages about what interests underlie the other side's position.[45] (Of course, we have honed this skill for years by obsessing for days on end about what our boyfriend meant when he said, *Sometimes I just need some alone time,* or the like).

While we are tooting our own horns, let's face it—Sisters are generally better than men at negotiating without the *intrusion of egos*.[46] We can use our knowledge of the uncontrollable testosterone-laden necessity for control and winning by letting the other side speak first and last if they want to, complimenting them if possible, and making meaningless concessions that will make them feel like they won so that we can win on the important issues.[47]

What about the hours? Are the stories about lawyers who practice corporate law having to sleep under their desks for days at a time truth or urban legend?

— Sidebar —

Certainly you've heard the one about the corporate attorney in New York City who thought he'd save a bundle by literally moving into his office. His residency went unnoticed for months, because it is not unusual for many corporate attorneys to keep extra clothing and personal items in the office. And with the big firms providing showers and sundries for all-nighters, you really don't have to go home all that often. As rumor has it, the partners eventually got wind of the homeless associate and promptly fired the guy.

Moral of the story: although the firm wants you to *live* there; don't take it literally.

Most corporate **Sisters** would agree that their hours are very similar to that of litigators on a yearly basis, but much more cyclical. In the heat of a big deal, you will not be brushing your teeth in your own sink very often. But if you are in between deals, you do have a lot of downtime to surf eBay and take long lunches, while litigation hours seem to be a bit steadier overall. And here's a little P.S. for you—if your dream is to someday go to the promised land of in-house attorneys, many headhunters report that you stand a better chance of getting this type of opportunity after practicing corporate law, rather than after a career in litigation.

IF YOU DON'T GO TO COURT, ARE YOU A LAWYER?

As a corporate lawyer, the conversation at your Thanksgiving dinner table may sound something like the following scenario.

Dad: *Sweetie, I got a ticket at the corner of Main and Church, and I swear, that light was as green as a tree. Can you help me out?*
Corporate **Sister**: *Sorry dad, I don't do that type of law.*

Mom: *Honey, am I entitled to unemployment benefits if I got fired for showing up late last week because the sample sale didn't even start until noon?*
Corporate **Sister**: *Sorry Mom, I don't do that type of law.*

Younger Wayward Brother: *Dude, I swear, someone planted that bag of [insert vice] in my college dorm room when the narcs searched my place. Can you help me out?*
Corporate **Sister**: *Sorry, kid, I don't do that type of law.*

Grandma Edna: *I'm going to meet my maker any day now. Can my granddaw-tah, the lawyer, probate my estate?*
Corporate **Sister**: *Sorry Grandma, I don't do that type of law.*

Aunt Doris: Can I sue the donut guy because I fell on a sheet of ice outside of his shop?
Corporate Sister: *Sorry Aunt Doris, I don't do that type of law.*

Dad, Mom, Brother, Grandma, Aunt (together): *Well, what kind of law do you do???*

Welcome to the mysterious world of transactional law, where opening statements, evidentiary objections, and jury analysts are as foreign to us as the phrase *too skinny* (for most of us, anyway). Sure, you use your law degree, but in a much different way.

It is hard to precisely define what *transactional law* means, other than to say that it encompasses everything besides litigation. One day you may be researching, the next you may be writing advice letters, and three weeks from now you may be drafting a deal document. Of course, many specialties encompass both transactional and litigation type work. Take, for example, intellectual property. While some IP lawyers may go to court and fight over patents, there are others who simply will review or draft applications for patents. It's important to find out before taking such a job how much litigation versus transactional work you can expect to do.

While we can't go into detail about every type of transactional or corporate substantive area, here is a quick summary of the tasks you may encounter.

Research and Writing

Sorry, Sisters. You can't get away from this mundane task as a Newbie associate just because you don't go to court. But the research will be different. Oftentimes, the issues posed are much more discrete and will become the basis of an opinion rendered to a client, rather than being incorporated into some sort of motion with annoying Bluebook citations all over the place. Also, the sources of your research are generally more defined than *all federal law.* Instead, you may be referred to a specific state corporate law or better yet, the specific corporate treatise that summarizes most of the laws and theories on point. So you can't kiss the library (and your deity, the librarian) goodbye forever, but you certainly won't be moving into the cubicle next door to Joe Litigator in the stacks.

Let Us Give You Some Advice

While litigation is all about living in the past (tell us what happened and let us see how we can put a nice spin on that story), transactional law is much more prospective. Thus, many transactional lawyers spend a good deal of their time writing advice letters for their clients either explaining the law, evaluating the legality of a proposed action, or rendering an opinion about the best way to do something. An advice letter requires complete attention to detail and the ability to explain complicated matters in a manner that second graders can understand.

You will also be surprised at how easy and basic drafting these letters can be (particularly when they are littered with caveats such as, *It seems/appears that; It is unclear whether, draft, and preliminary findings*—or when you use the motherload of CYA devices, the [*brackets*]). Remember, things that seem quite intuitive to you, oh clever Newbie, may indeed seem quite complex to a humble nonattorney.

The Printers

If your clients are public corporations, there are certain disclosures they need to make to their owners, the public, or potential investors if they are about to take some sort of material action that will affect the company. The action is documented into something called a *prospectus*, which is put onto paper by a professional printer. A typical public deal requires anywhere from 10,000 to 20,000 copies of the preliminary prospectus (known as the *red herring*) and 5,000 to 10,000 copies of the final prospectus.[48]

When a prospectus is near completion, the lawyers, bankers, and senior management of the parties all go to the *printing party* (a misnomer because it's a far cry from any party you have ever attended), which may become their home for several days. This *party* is the last meeting where the parties must hammer out all of the fine details of the deal. Because the printer's party is very expensive and companies are eager to move to the next stages of the deal, there is an extraordinary amount of pressure put on the parties to finalize EVERYTHING before leaving the premises. This means getting a room full of lawyers and other anal-retentive types to agree on commas, language, and grammar (not to mention substance)—a task tantamount to the Israeli-Palestinian peace negotiations.

On the plus side, some refer to the printers' office as the *country club prison*. It is fully equipped with showers, all the food you can eat (look out LASS, here we come), and other amenities to accommodate locked-in-until-you're-done sessions.[49] The best restaurants cater to printers, and M&M's always seem to appear on the table just when you're having a sugar low.[50] And don't overlook the pillows, cots, pool tables, stocked bars, and pinball machines for those 3 a.m. breaks.[51] It's not a practice we're proud of as a profession, but the only way to get some things hammered out is the promise of going home once it's all over.

SO WHAT'S THE BIG DEAL?

The *Big Deal* is probably the bread and butter (we just can't help talking about food) of most transactional practices. Although each firm does deals in their particular fashion, here's a rundown of what you might expect to encounter as a Newbie.

The Process

One day you will get the call that you are on the Deal Team—you must learn to like (or at least tolerate) the Team, as you will spend more time with them as the deal progresses than with your husband on your honeymoon. At most firms, your name will then be put on something called the *Player's List*, which contains the contact information (including, sadly, all home numbers) for each warm body helping to get the deal done—including attorneys and staff at your firm and the opposing firm, the client, and most of the time, the investment bankers and the accountants. This list is critical because as a Newbie associate, you will be expected to make many distributions during your tenure on the Deal, and you don't want to have to search for addresses each and every time.

If the deal involves public entities, most firms require you to refer to the parties, even in private, by their Secret Insiders Names (SINs), which range from the obscure to the ludicrous, and oftentimes borrow the first letter of the real names of the parties. One **Sister** recalled that she had to stop herself from chuckling about the Eggs and Mustard SINs (*aka* Exxon-Mobil deal). But it's no laughing matter if you use the real names—any leaks about a public deal can result in serious insider trading allegations or killing a deal—both sins in themselves. Armed with your Player's List and SINs, the process usually proceeds as follows.

DUE DILIGENCE

Sorry to disappoint those litigators taking refuge in corporate law, but the dreaded due diligence is still required in this type of practice. Transactional due diligence generally involves reading through mounds and mounds of legal documents from your client and the target or acquiring company. It is your job to read each and every document and summarize your football field of boxes into a concise due diligence memorandum. You will no doubt fall into a coma during this mundane process of spitting back information like a parrot, yet it is critical to the process. The idea is that you need to know as much about your client and the other company as possible, in order to structure the deal and fine tune the terms and conditions of the contract underlying the deal.

The hard part about this process is that as a Newbie, you sort of don't know exactly what you're looking for, so most of us will parrot back more, rather than less, in the early years, and our due diligence memorandum looks more like a treatise. The irony is, of course, when you finally get enough experience to spot the issues, the due diligence dregs are delegated to someone junior to you, so the cycle continues. Unfortunately, it seems like it's the only way we really learn the ropes in this business.

NEGOTIATION AND TERM SHEETS

Once the *players* understand what the parties are about, the fun begins with the rainmakers hammering out the terms of the Deal. Everything from the economics to what to do with the employees and real estate, among many other details, must be defined. The succinct version of the basic elements of the agreement is documented in what is called a *term sheet*, which is usually a two-columned list with each issue on the left side and how it will be resolved on the right side.

During the negotiation process, there will be investment bankers and accountants on the deal to help you out with the scary numbers. These people are the ones who actually price the deals and figure out the accounting impacts. Again, while you'll need a very rudimentary knowledge of what's *good* and *bad* accounting for your clients, you don't need an MBA (although it couldn't hurt).

And while we're talking about nonlawyers, here's a doozy. Did you know that while law firms are generally paid by the hour for our time working on the deals (with an occasional premium if the deal is successful), investment bankers take a cut (a certain percentage) of the deal if it closes? Thus, the bankers have a perverse incentive to make a deal happen quickly—even if it's not the best deal possible—while the lawyers may laboriously stretch the deal out, investigating all possible angles and leaving no stones unturned.

As a Newbie associate, you will feel like you spend your whole life waiting. You wait while the rainmakers hammer out the terms before you draft the term sheet; you wait for the secretary to process changes on the drafts; you wait for the paralegals to conform and proof changes; and then, you wait for the senior associates to review your work. It's like a nightmare trip to the overbooked Botox doc's office (but the wait lasts much, much longer).

You will spend almost as many hours on the partner's low couch on conference calls as you do waiting. You will be shocked and amazed by how much time you spend listening to calls that only remotely touch upon your responsibilities of the Deal. Every time anything is spoken about the Deal, the partner will routinely call you into his office to listen in. It's really a shame because oftentimes you have way too much work to lounge around on the low couch daydreaming about what you're going to eat at 3 a.m., but it will happen over and over again.

Why subject you to the conference call torture? (It is possible that the partners view it as part of the training and development process, but we doubt it.) More likely, they just want to make sure they have a second warm body there to take notes so that they don't miss anything (particularly when they walk out of the office to talk to their friends, leaving you sitting there to respond in your best imitation of the partner's voice). While you may be inclined to become the Picasso of doodles during these calls, your efforts are probably better spent just taking dictation like a secretary. Also, we suspect that the partners want you on the call so if there are any tasks to be done resulting from the call, they don't have to explain it again.

After spending hours and hours singing the due diligence blues, sinking into the low couch, and churning edits, you may find yourself with serious homicidal tendencies to *kill the Deal*. There is no bigger cause for celebration amongst Newbie associates than when they find out that a *Deal died*. While the partners will mourn its sudden passing (mostly because the firm reaps a premium for completed deals), you will go out and celebrate just as Dorothy did after the Wicked Witch of the West evaporated. But before you get too crazy and throw away all of the deceased's belongings, a word to the wise—deals may actually rise from the dead, in which case you had better be prepared to deal with the resurrection.

DRAFTING CONTRACTS

Once the basic tenets of the Deal are struck, it's time to draft. Although we often start with a basic format and insert the pertinent terms of the deal, the creative possibilities are endless. A top-notch contract drafter is all about predicting the future for her client. Unlike litigation, where you are brought aboard to react once a problem arises, contract drafting requires you to predict potential problems in advance and to provide written remedies that work in the best interest of your client. Once you've had enough experience, drafting becomes an art, and *wordsmithing* or *tweaking* becomes, dare we say it, almost fun. As geeky as it sounds, comma placement and language formulas can change the dynamics of an entire document, and picking up on these little nuances becomes sport.

One of the most important aspects of drafting is which party has *control* of the document. This is usually the party that scribes the first draft and therefore uses its own forms and style. Wearing the drafter's shoes has its advantages. First, you are using your form, with which you are already familiar and comfortable. Second, you have the first opportunity to draft the document in favor of your clients. Once the other side receives the initial draft, it is their job to review, digest, and deal with Markup Madness (the MUMs). The MUMs are the heart of the drafting process.

As an aside, if you want to identify the dinosaurs at your firm (or those people who are over age 40), they will be the people calling the changed document a *redline*. The term comes from the process used in the *old days* whereby paralegals would underline by hand, in red, all of the changes that had been made to a document.

In the olden days, the MUMs practice involved painstakingly inserting carrots with bubbles filled to the brim (and oftentimes overflowing down the sides of each and every margin of the page) with edits and deletions. Trying to read and decipher where the changes belonged was more difficult than finding Waldo. Nowadays, most firms use all sorts of advanced word processing programs that will show each and every change in a neat and concise manner right inside the text of the document (called a *blackline*) that has been made to a document so we don't waste our precious time comparing drafts for changes.

As a Newbie, your life will also revolve around the world of *scheduling*. Sadly, we're not talking about mani and pedi appointments. Schedules are attachments to the main contract that carve out exceptions to the warranties or representations so that the contract doesn't get too long. Oftentimes a relatively short contract will have hundreds of pages of schedules attached to it. For example, a typical contract may state that it has no outstanding debt, except as provided on Schedule A, which in turn lists all of the banks to whom a company owes money.

Sounds simple enough, right? The process gets complicated, however, when there are dozens and sometimes even hundreds of schedules attached, and each time a schedule is added or deleted, your whole darn document and all exhibits need to be conformed. While it sounds like paralegal work, ultimately you, oh holy Newbie, are responsible for the schedules.

CLOSING

You would think that once a contract is signed, the show is over, let's go celebrate, right? Unfortunately, there's still work to be done. Just because the parties may agree to the terms and conditions among themselves, some deals will require regulatory approval or some other condition to be satisfied before it's a *done deal*, so to speak. The deal will be consummated, as they say, at the closing. Your job as a Newbie associate is to yet again revisit and update the documents and make sure everything else in the world of your deal is in order. Sometimes preparation for the closing requires almost as much effort as negotiating the contract itself, so be prepared for some more nights sleeping on the floor. However, there is nothing finer than witnessing the culmination of all of your hard work at the closing, not to mention seeing your name in teensy-itsy-bitsy print in the local newspaper (which may oftentimes include obscure publications like *The Wall Street Journal* or *The New York Times*).

POST-CLOSE EUPHORIA

Post-close euphoria is the dream of every corporate attorney. Your deal is done, the parties are happy, the bankers are rich, and the partners buy another sports car. As for you, Newbies are oftentimes invited to the lavish closing dinners where no bottle is too expensive to celebrate the monumental task that has just been accomplished (not to mention the end of your isolation from the outside world). And just when you think it can't get any better, you get the acrylic deal toy—a symbol of your fine accomplishments. Maybe you will show up for work the next day, maybe you won't— basically, no one cares because they know you've been averaging 300 hours a month and earning your keep. Time to slack off, eBay shop, and turn off your brain for at least another few days, until the partners discover that you are yet again *available* for work— and then welcome back to the due diligence blues.

The Deal Team

Now that we've demystified the process, let's turn to the characters that become your family during the deal. It turns out that most of the time, the Deal Team is organized just like the mafia. Here's a summary of the players who will become your partners in crime (no pun intended) from the top down.

THE DON

This is the rainmaker who brought in the client and runs the show. In the mafia, the *Don* decides who gets made, who gets whacked, and who receives the largest share of points (*percentage of income*) depending upon how he runs the family business. He's concerned with the big picture decisions, like putting a contract out on a snitch, but rarely bothers with the details of how it is done, what time of day, or who does the dirty work. Same story with the partner running your deal.

The head *honcho* concentrates upon negotiating with the boss on the other side of the table and appeasing the client. He wants the work done and is either unconcerned or unaware of what it takes to turn the documents. (Although we believe it is most likely that he suffers from partnership-induced amnesia, since a short ten or fifteen years or so earlier he was a baby associate on a deal and knew first-hand the time it took to conform all the schedules once a change was made.)

THE UNDERBOSS

Next in command is the junior partner on the deal, or the *underboss* in Gotti-lingo. The underboss deals with all of the technicalities, like whether a hit will be carried out by a shot to the head while in bed with the mistress or at the lake with a cement block tied to the snitch's ankle. He locates the black Lincoln Town Car with a trunk big enough to transport the rat and devises the details of how it will be cleaned out after the big event. He's got hands-on control of the show and is there for all of the action, including the actual hit. Your junior partner plays the very same role. He or she is shoulder to shoulder with you in the conference room 24/7 to oversee all of the details, to guarantee that no deal point goes unchecked, and to verify that all of the documents work together to achieve the intended result for your client.

THE CAPO

The senior (usually Bubble) associate functions just like a *capo* (the slang Italian term for the leader of a crew). He, too, is involved 24/7, but to supervise the foot soldiers and make certain they are carrying out the underboss's instructions precisely as given. Likewise, your senior associate on the deal supervises the dredge work of a crew of baby associates, paralegals, and secretaries actually doing the MUMs, editing, and proofing of the documents.

THE CONSIGLIORE

These are the specialists that the underbosses and *capos* turn to for advice outside of their expertise. Many corporate deals involve extremely discrete and detailed knowledge of subject areas outside of their control, such as tax, real estate, ERISA, and estate issues. Strapped for time in order to execute a timely hit, the *capos* will turn to the specialists to get the job done in an efficient manner. The *consigliore* relish their roles in the job because as soon as their advice is dispensed, they disappear from the transaction and will deny having anything to do with it if something goes wrong.

THE FOOT SOLDIERS

The foot soldiers are everybody else on the deal, including baby associates, paralegals, and secretaries. As the bottom-level members of the family, soldiers must remain on-call every hour of the day and carry out instructions down to the smallest detail without questioning the orders. These are the guys who do the actual shake down; who lug the body from the trunk of the car to the river's edge; and, who do all the spring cleaning (hiding of evidence) after the hit. As a Newbie you'll play the same role (except, hopefully, for the hiding of evidence part). You'll probably be responsible for only one piece of the deal and may not even understand exactly how it fits into the big picture. Nevertheless, you'll markup, edit, proof, and otherwise do every piece of grunt work associated with your little piece of the big deal pie.

KNOW THE LINGO

The longer you practice corporate law, the larger your corporatese dictionary becomes. If you haven't noticed already, lawyers love to show the world just how smart they are by speaking in as many big words, catchphrases, and metaphors as possible. Following is a list of a few of our favorites, along with their translations—just to get you started.

SMART Word or Phrase	Translation
Pari Passu	Each party will be treated the same (*i.e.*, if one of the parties must pay a penalty of $5/7^{th}$ of its revenues, so must the other party).
Most Favored Nation Clause	Not an international doctrine at all. It simply means that if there are a range of possible outcomes, your client will be treated as good as the party that benefits the most from the deal.
"I am marginally competent, but…" "Call me thick, but…"	This is part of the *humbling* negotiation tactic. First, you put yourself down, and the phrase that follows *but*—is what you demand is reasonable on behalf of your client.
"I hate to split hairs here…"	A lead in used when you are negotiating minor, but important, details on behalf of your client.
"I need to check with the client on this one." "I have no authority to make this decision." or "that's a business call."	Used when there's a major decision you can't make as a lawyer. Sometimes used for procrastination purposes as well.
"I hate to beat a dead horse, but…."	Used as a lead in when you won't let something drop, but you know you're becoming annoying and sounding like a broken record.
"I'm sorry, but perhaps I'm not making myself clear…."	Used when you have to explain things in second grade language to stupid opposing counsel. Also used sarcastically if the opposing counsel won't listen to you.

"It's going to be a sin in Leviticus when…."	Meaning that nothing will change your mind about a certain topic, short of a biblical sin.
"With all due respect…"	Usually used by litigators in the court-room as a sign of respect to the judge, but here it's used in a condescending fashion when addressing opposing counsel right before you disagree 100% with his or her position.
"I will not negotiate with myself…"	When you have made an offer and the other side wants you to sweeten the offer, but does nothing to respond to your initial offer.
"I'm from Missouri here, so…"	Missouri is the *Show Me* state, so this phrase is used when you think opposing counsel is lying and you want them to justify their claims.
"That clause/issue is radioactive" or "gives the client heartburn."	Used when the client is highly sensitive about a particular issue.
"She's a lightweight."	Referring to an attorney who is too young, junior, or stupid to be a good negotiator—never said directly to an attorney's face.
And the motherload of catchphrases… "I just don't understand."	The most popular stalling device when you don't know how to respond. Buys you time to think of other arguments so the other side has to repeat itself. Also works when you're too lazy to figure out something yourself. Do not overuse, because everyone sees through it.

TRANSACTIONAL BLISS

While it's not an easier life than litigation, in the grand scheme of things, it can be more satisfying because transactional lawyers help their clients accomplish an agreement from which everyone benefits at the end of the process. The hours tend to be longer on a cyclical basis, but you appreciate the Post-Close Euphoria and have more time to catch your breath in between deals. At the end of the day, even if you're doing corporate law and sleeping on the floor, at least all the niceties—the big closing dinner, a tad of notoriety in the local law journal, and best of all, the acrylic metal of honor (deal toy or plaque) make it worth the effort.

■ ■ ■

12

Finding the Right Fit

-sisterly specialties-

a s early as first grade, it hits you like a ton of bricks—the dreaded Sunday night blues. After a perfect weekend of sleeping in, hanging out with friends, and generally de-stressing, at around 3 p.m. Sunday, you suddenly find yourself in the shadow of the very, very dark new workweek cloud. The thought of another grueling 40–100 hour stint in the office sends you into an impenetrable funk, which can only be cured by polishing off an entire pint of *Ben & Jerry's*. The best recipe for battling the blues is finding something you like to do (although when it comes right down to it, does anyone really like to work?).

FINDING YOUR GLASS SLIPPER

Most of us are familiar with the made-for-TV movie about *Cinderella*. In this *Disneyesque* version of the tale, our little heroine has an extreme makeover before the ball, where she sadly loses a Manolo-like glass number. As fate has it, she finds her Prince, and even more importantly, her missing designer shoe. What you may not know is that the G-rated version leaves out some morbid details from the original Grimm brothers' story, namely, that the

Did you know that **Sisters** have been known to subject their poor piggies to padding, taping, collagen injections, and the most egregious act of all, amputation of pieces of the piggies that don't quite fit into the pointy torture devices?[52]

evil step-sisters hacked off pieces of their feet so that they could fit into the coveted glass slipper.

So why are we talking about fairy tales again when we're supposed to be talking about law? As women, we can all relate to our never-ending search for the perfect pair of shoes. While some of us will do just about anything to sport those narrow-tipped hooker heels that hurt like hell, those of us with experience know that nothing good can come from wearing them for too long. Law practice is no different. You must resist the temptation to choose a path that doesn't fit right, just because it looks or sounds good.

The Search for Your Solemates

How will you know if you have found your Prince Charming? If you glaze over into a stupor after five minutes of listening to a **Sister** describe her particular practice area, cross it off of your list. All those expensive career consultants will tell you to explore the *Color of Your Parachute* by ascertaining your strengths and weaknesses, your likes and dislikes, and your ultimate goals. Of course, for most of us, all that touchy-feely psychoanalysis goes right out the door once we get a glimpse of the six-inch high *Gucci* heels. While we know how hard it is to resist the temptation (since we didn't), you should think long and hard about harmonizing your career goals with your personal aspirations from the outset. Sure, your expensive spa visits and nasty *Hermes* habit scream *I need to earn the big bucks*, but in the long-term, you may need a practice area that is rugrat-friendly.

All that being said, the true problem is that you don't know if the shoe will fit until you've had a chance to try it on. The best you can do is educate yourself about what's out there and talk to as many people as possible about what they do (believe us, most **Sisters** are not shy about talking and complaining about their jobs). If you don't feel like becoming the sounding board for others' incessant bantering, here's a quick and dirty summary of what you should consider.

GENERAL PRACTITIONERS VERSUS SPECIALISTS

Your first consideration should be general practitioner (GP) or specialist? Forgive us for obsessing about food again, but if eating the same fat-free turkey sandwich on whole wheat toast (no mayo) every single day for lunch is comforting, becoming a specialist may be your calling. On the other hand, if you suffer even a tad from ADD (as most **Sisters** do) and prefer Mexican, Chinese, Italian, Kosher, and Indian for lunch on Monday, Tuesday, Wednesday, Thursday, and Friday, respectively, then experiencing all of the different spices of a general practice may be more your speed. (Indulge us in exploring these two areas.)

Wearing the Cross-Trainers

GP's are the cross-trainers of law practice. As most of you well know, these are the shoes designed for the super-duper athlete who dabbles in different sports on various terrains, yet is not high performing in any one of them. Like cross-trainers, GP's represent clients in a variety of practice areas, but are not experts on any one topic. For example, GP litigators will represent clients in a variety of subject matters, whereas GP corporate associates will work on all aspects of clients' deals. Of course, the true GP's are the hang-a-shingle lawyers who handle run-of-the-mill legal issues, such as drafting wills, quickie divorces, setting up corporations, and handling DWI's. This is a tough gig though, because in most cases, it's about volume over deep pockets, so you'll need to hit the ground looking for clients.

Sidebar

We note that many GPs have mastered the art of protecting their rears by calling in the specialists while still raking in the dough. You see, when they refer the matter out, they will negotiate a *referral fee*. Alternatively, they may *oversee* the specialists, which allows them to collect for doing nothing while making sure the specialists do not run away with their clients.

Wearing the Spinning Shoes

Specialists are practitioners who wear the indoor cycling footwear known as spin shoes, which have clips that fit into the pedals of your stationary bike so you don't go flying into oblivion when you are riding on the handlebars at high speeds. If you try to wear these clunky shoes anywhere other than on the bike, you will fall and almost kill yourself. Similarly, legal specialists devote themselves to one area of the law and can't do much else.

In reality, almost everyone is somewhat of a specialist these days. Everything in law has become so technical that there's not enough time in the day to become an expert on everything (and, at the very least, it's nearly impossible to serve as a smooth corporate lawyer and a fierce litigator).

If you are a specialty litigator, you can usually reap the benefits of your prior work product, because nine times out of ten, you can reuse some portion of your previous work on a current case. After all, the law governing sexual harassment, for example, doesn't change because a different horny male is accused of groping his secretary.

Transactional specialists also have a good gig as cogs in a very big wheel. For example, if you specialize in tax, ERISA, real estate, or other ancillary transactional work, you will only have to work on one teensy-intsy-weensy portion of monster deals. The dredge work of turning documents, sitting at the printers, and babysitting paralegals as they number and renumber endless exhibits is saved for the corporate generalists.

Of course, the downside (isn't there always?) of specializing is that you know a lot of information about a minute topic. Almost every time someone asks you what seems like an easy legal question unrelated to your field, your tepid response will have to be *I'm sorry, I don't practice that type of law.* This particularly upsets the cab drivers looking to get out of traffic tickets or your mother wanting to sue her dry cleaner for destroying her suede coat.

CORPORATE GOVERNANCE LAW: GO SOX!

The new millennium is all about SOX and we don't mean the things keeping your piggies toasty or the Curse of the Bambino. The *Sarbanes-Oxley Act* (SOX) was passed in response to the collapse of Enron and the succeeding corporate scandals. Corporate lawyers could not have dreamed up a better law to keep them busy. Not a day goes by that we don't read about the Security and Exchange Commission or some stock exchange issuing or proposing rules interpreting SOX or blowing the whistle on another crooked executive. Because the SOX penalty scares the socks off of executives, corporate lawyers are spending more and more of their time counseling companies and their boards of directors about what is and is not kosher behavior.

SOX law will give you exposure to the top Muckety-Mucks of public companies (okay, really the partner you work for will, but sitting in on conference calls with them and drafting all the pertinent documents counts), as well as advance knowledge of great corporate scandals before they hit the *Wall Street Journal*. If you can deal with handholding neurotic executives and directors and cleaning up the aftermath of questionable behavior, perhaps you should try on these socks for size.

CRIMINAL LAW: I SWEAR I DIDN'T DO IT LAW

Sisters who actually practice this type of law report that there is nothing routine or predictable about a criminal lawyer's day. Some days you may be negotiating a person's life behind bars, while other days you may be bargaining over a traffic ticket.

Aside from white-collar defense lawyers, most criminal lawyers can forget fancy dinners at the hottest restaurants shmoozing for work. Your clients are either:

- alleged law-breakers of the most heinous kind (who usually have no money, but manage to scrape up a measly amount from their families to pay your fees) or
- the State (who also doesn't have any money, but manages to scrape up a measly amount from taxpayers to pay your salary). If you represent the State, you will never have to worry about keeping busy, but if you are in private practice, how do you bring in the clients if your social circles don't involve *alleged* kleptomaniacs, drug dealers, and parolees? Sadly, the answer is usually word of mouth—from one *alleged* to another, that is.

One **Sister** told us that she built up her entire practice from a little note engraved on the bathroom wall at the local men's jail by her first client. (What was actually written on the wall still remains a mystery to this day.)

Even if you are not interested in making criminal law your career, it is one of the best foundations for litigation. Unlike any other practice area, it seems that criminal lawyers are thrown into the fire and allowed to do more court work than any other specialty. Of course, you also have to deal with unpleasant subject matters, at times unsavory characters, and the chance that your name will wind up in places worse than the prison bathroom wall.

ENTERTAINMENT LAW: REPRESENTING AMERICA'S ROYALTY

Imagine all this in a day's work: negotiating the terms of Brad Pitt's film project; discovering the next Harry Potter-type author; and preparing product endorsement deals between Britney Spears and Tampax tampons. Well, if you believe this is the typical life of an entertainment lawyer, you have either watched far too many episodes of *Arli$$* or you must still be in law school. Perhaps one day you'll actually rub elbows with some of America's *royalty* in Hollywood, but the truth of the matter is that most entertainment lawyers are simply commercial or corporate lawyers who service needy, egotistical, artsy-fartsy clients with little to no business acumen. These clients (many of whom are unknowns) typically demand constant attention from everyone taking a piece of their pot, including, but not limited to, their business managers, agents, parents, shrinks, trainers, kabbalah or Scientology instructors, and of course, you, their lawyer.

Entertainment law is also broader than what one may think. It not only involves blockbuster films, but also music, books, television, theater, sports, resorts, and casinos. Entertainment lawyers represent not only big shot movie stars, but also musicians, musical bands, filmmakers, producers, directors, opera companies, and dance companies to name a few. Making it in this field requires you to learn the lingo and the ins and outs of the industry, acquire a thick skin, hone up on how deals are reached, and most importantly, get in good with the right contacts. Sometimes the old saying, *It's not what you know, but who you know* couldn't be more true.

You will also require more than cursory knowledge about contract law, intellectual property, commercial transactions, secured financial transactions, estate planning, collective bargaining agreements, union requirements, employee benefits, and tax law because it's all about heavy negotiation and doing deals on behalf of your client. If this list of requirements doesn't scare or bore you to death, and you have the patience to babysit colossal egos, perhaps you too can court America's royalty.

FAMILY LAW:
CAN'T LIVE WITH THEM, BUT CAN'T SHOOT THEM LAW

Sure, you may be hooked on one or two good soap operas in which sex, marriage, adulterous affairs, and ultimately divorce are part of a vicious cycle that keeps you coming back for more. In the real world, however, divorce law—the bread and butter of most family law practices—can be even more emotionally draining than criminal law. But with divorce rates in the good old U.S. of A. topping 50%, job security will never be an issue in this field. Along with the psychological torture of dealing with the highly personal issues surrounding sour marriages, you also have to deal with child and spousal support, visitation, family custody, dividing property, prenuptials, and postnuptials.

On the upside, however, the world of family law extends beyond divorce. Family lawyers will handle guardianships for the elderly, children, infirmed and mentally disabled who cannot take care of themselves, domestic and foreign adoptions, termination of parental rights, and establishment of paternity. In addition, with the increased hoopla over same-sex marriages and this group's expanding use of fertility treatments and adoptions, the range of issues facing family lawyers continues to grow.

On the practical side, most family law attorneys spend their days counseling clients, making court appearances, and working up their cases. However, it seems that nine out of ten cases settle on the courthouse steps.

IMMIGRATION LAW: THE INTERNATIONAL BABYSITTER

Do you get teary eyed when you see the Statue of Liberty? Were you glued to the tube during the Elian Gonzalez saga? If so, then immigration law may be your passport to happiness. This area of law has really taken off recently as foreign employees are increasingly employed in this fine country due to a growth in global business operations. *There is actually an individual behind every piece of paper I turn,* says one **Sister**, who feels double gratification when she arranges for a foreign employee to come to work for her U.S.-based corporate clients. Many of the smaller and solo immigration firms devote the majority of their practices to representing individuals, thereby offering young lawyers tremendous hands-on responsibility. Saving clients from deportation, reuniting family members, and helping clients' fulfill their dreams of living and working in the U.S. is the greatest challenge and the best reward.

While sharing the American dream is a noble cause, you better have a whole lot of patience and compassion. Talk about an administrative nightmare. The vast majority of the work is document-driven and bureaucracy intensive. With people's lives and corporations' livelihoods at stake, clients are demanding, work is time-sensitive, and the pressure can be unrelenting. These *international babysitters* process heaps and heaps of paperwork to accomplish their tasks. With the crackdown on U.S. immigration policies (along with convoluted regulations hastily adopted after 9/11), it seems that immigration lawyers are in higher demand now more than ever.

While you won't get to sit in on the U.N. sessions, you may receive some cool chachkas from foreign countries from your clients. If that isn't enticing enough, consider this—your immigration clients will be deeply appreciative of your work and oftentimes promise to name their first born after you. Of course, the best perk of all is no opposing counsel to yell at you or send hate mail everyday.

EMPLOYMENT LAW: WORKPLACE SOAP OPERAS

With Americans spending more time in the office than at home, the workplace is tantamount to an episode of *Survivor*, in which greed, laziness, jealousy, anger, and sexual tension ultimately leads to a deterioration of alliances. Unlike *Survivor*, however, when someone is kicked off the island (*i.e.*, terminated in the office), they don't just jog off into the sunset with their torch and appear on the CBS *Early Show* the next day to talk about it. Instead, they file multimillion dollar lawsuits against their employers and go on the *Howard Stern* show to badmouth anyone who has harmed them.

Historically, **Sisters** have been attracted to this field because employment laws were intended to protect discrete and insular minorities—most notably, us. Oddly enough, most wind up representing management and advising employers against claims of sexual harassment and other distasteful employment law violations.

While most employment arrangements are *at-will* (you can be hired or fired for no reason or any reason at all), there are a plethora of federal, state, and local laws that chip away at the at-will doctrine. With all of these laws and regulations, it's pretty hard to fire anyone (short of their committing triple homicide on the premises) without risking a lawsuit these days, so you will never be without work.

Speaking of job security, if you practice this type of law you will wear the golden handcuffs for life as your employer will be terrified of getting rid of you because this is what you do for a living. You see, most employment law actions contain every cause of action under the sun, even though some, if not all of them, are not actionable. No matter how far-out the allegations, nine times out of ten the employer cries mercy and settles for big bucks. So the last thing your employer wants to face is a lawsuit by a person who is keenly aware of all of the annoying ways in which employees can extort money from their employers, not to mention, all the employment laws the employer has violated. (We know what you are thinking. How can employment law firms not abide by the same laws in which they advise their clients to comply with each and everyday? It's no different than the shoemaker's kids who wear ratty shoes.)

On the upside, doing discovery is more fun than reading the *Enquirer*. One **Sister** will never forget the key exhibit in a case in which her client was accused of sexual harassment for whipping out his pee-pee in front of the plaintiff. In the deposition, after the plaintiff testified that the accused was circumcised, the **Sister** quickly disposed of the case when she introduced a glossy 8" x 10" picture of her client's penis—which in fact was wearing the old turtleneck—to prove the plaintiff was lying.

BANKRUPTCY LAW: DISCOVERING THAT SOMEONE HAS MORE IRRESPONSIBLE SPENDING HABITS THAN YOU

For all you who have thought of filing bankruptcy to wipe out your student loans, forget about it! Nondischargeable, ladies. But instead of joining the debtors, why not represent them? Bankruptcy lawyers are rarely hungry for work, even in good economies.

As a little background, the purpose of the bankruptcy system is to give individuals and organizations an opportunity to resolve and reorder their financial affairs while providing protection to their creditors when they cannot meet their financial obligations.

Since every legal relationship between the debtor and each creditor must be resolved in the bankruptcy case, these **Sisters** play a multitude of roles, touching on almost every substantive area of law. Even though you may have an opportunity to shine in court early on (bankruptcy lawyers find themselves in court at very junior levels because there are so many preliminary motions to be made that don't require the big Muckety-Mucks to show up), you will still get the CRAPS just as often. You will have to hone up on commercial financing laws (to secure financing to debtors continuing to operate), mergers and acquisitions law (to structure asset sales), labor and employment law (for employee retention issues), Uniform Commercial Code/secured transactions law (to understand creditors' rights to the pie), as well as a little bit of tax, real estate, landlord/tenant, environmental, and domestic relations law. Because every aspect of the debtor's financial life is unique, there is never a dull (or down) moment.[53]

The juicy part of the practice, of course, is taking a sneak peak into someone else's spending habits. Debtors will try to hide assets, repay preferred creditors, and fraudulently convey property immediately before they file. It's your job to play Sherlock Holmes and smoke out the missing goods.

TAX LAW: THE PROCTOLOGY OF LAW PRACTICE

Ben Franklin had it right when he said in 1789, "But in this world nothing can be said to be certain, except death and taxes." This still rings true more than 200 years later. The Internal Revenue Code is the *mother* of all statutes. Like proctologists, tax lawyers aren't necessarily fun or glamorous, but it's a person that we all need at some point in our lives and their services will always be in high demand. Tax law is not for the intellectually impaired (translation—you sort of need to be a tax-geek to get into all the statutes and regulations). All of those dense books lining the bookshelves are not just for show. These complex, highly technical, ever-changing rules keep Sisters on their toes. As a result, tax attorneys have become increasingly specialized. They are called upon (usually by corporate lawyers) to assess the tax consequences of a par-

ticular part of a transaction. In fact, they are one of the first players on the deal team who helps to structure the transactions in a
tax-efficient manner (and are also called upon at the eleventh
hour of a closing in case the structure is not working out).

Tax issues arise in every discipline—individual disputes with the
IRS, business transactions, estates and trusts, employee benefits,
settlements, and even family law. At large firms, tax attorneys have
the opportunity to handle everything from structured finance, to
mergers and acquisitions, to initial public offerings. On a day-to-
day basis, these lawyers spend a good deal of time keeping up with
changes in the law, advising clients on the effects of these changes,
and staying abreast of business developments.

If you suffer from an extreme form of *Cause and Effect Disorder* or
loved the logic questions on the LSAT that gave the majority of the
population the heeby-jeebies, navigating through the Code may
be your schtick. It involves solving intellectually challenging puz-
zles, detail-oriented research, and code-based legal analysis. You
will have to muddle through disjointed verbiage to solve some of
the problems, and an accounting or business degree, while not
required, can't hurt. In fact, many tax-Sisters actually go back to
school (yet again!) to receive an advanced degree (LL.M.) in taxation to round out their knowledge in this area. The good news?
Your day-to-day existence won't address unsavory human behavior. The bad news? Your human behavior becomes one and the
same with the tax treatises.

EMPLOYEE BENEFITS AND EXECUTIVE COMPENSATION LAW: PLAYING WITH OTHER PEOPLE'S MONEY

For Sisters who are interested in employment law issues, but have
no interest in public speaking or dealing with whiny clients all day,
consider employee benefits law—a hybrid of tax, corporate, securities, and employment law. For whatever reason, the top scholars in
this area, as well as the majority of practitioners, tend to be women.

This practice is about as *nichy* as it gets, but its subject matter is all near and dear to our hearts—protection of other people's compensation. Much of this practice involves interpreting complex rules and regulations under the *Employee Retirement Income Security Act of 1974* (ERISA), which was originally enacted to protect the funds of private pension plans that were being mismanaged (*i.e.*, embezzled). While many label this field as *ivory tower* (*i.e.*, no practical use whatsoever in the real world), it is pivotal to the deal process because for every corporate transaction, there are executives, employees, and employee benefit plans and assets that must negotiated.

ERISA attorneys are usually few and far between (did you know what they did before you went to law school?) and most seem to wind up in the field by default. The practice generally involves three jobs. First, for the socially challenged (or disgusted, as the case may be), it is all about research—ERISA attorneys bury their heads in the tax code to ensure that employee benefit plans are *qualified* (meaning they receive favorable tax treatment) and in the ERISA statute to ensure that the funds underlying plan assets are invested in kosher deals. Second, ERISA attorneys are transactional lawyers who deal with the employee-related benefits issues in big transactions. (Many of them used to be corporate attorneys themselves, but they saw the light when the ERISA kids went home at night with no further document turning duties). Third, and perhaps the sexiest (okay, it's all relative) part of their job, is the executive compensation component. Nothing better than finding out what all the big-wigs are earning and trying to negotiate and structure similar deals for your clients. Perhaps the toughest part of the job is keeping yourself from getting sick on the employment agreements once you see how much the greedy executives earn (which is never enough in their opinions) compared to your measly salary.

TRUSTS & ESTATES LAW: THE WORK THAT NEVER DIES

What better way to finish off a conversation about what you can do with your life than with death? While Trusts and Estates (T&E) lawyers don't have to deal with whiney clients (absent séances and resurrections), they do have to deal with the day-to-day drudgery of drafting highly technical documents designed to maximize dead people's estates and minimize taxes taken out of the same.

In summary, if you love eating bagels and lox at shiva calls or manicotti after wakes, if you'll die if you miss an episode of *Six Feet Under*, and most importantly, if technical legal drafting doesn't kill you, then consider a career in Trusts & Estates.

LIVING HAPPILY EVER AFTER

So, at the end of the *Disneyesque* version of Cinderella, we know that Cindy gets an Extreme Makeover, snags her Prince, finds the other half of her precious glass slippers, and never even gets so much as a blister from those nasty things. Of course, back here on earth, it is more likely that your first glass slippers will destroy your feet. Never fear, we won't leave your tired tootsies out to dry with all the other malcontent lawyers out there. Join us one last time as we put on our running shoes in our quest to find the pair of shoes that fits just right.

■ ■ ■

13

Wearing Running Shoes

-the great escape-

You shouldn't be surprised to learn that your relationship with your employer shares the same paradigm as your relationships with significant others. At the beginning, you are so smitten that a separation—or even worse, a total breakup—is completely unfathomable. Sadly, we know that at least 50% of all marriages end in divorce. The survival rate of your affair with your first legal employer is even bleaker—38% of new associates switched employers within the *first three years* of employment, and 60% of large firm associates changed jobs at least once in the *first five years* of practice.[54] And it seems that women tend to exercise their feminine prerogatives a bit more than the Y-Factor, with the attrition rates for women being five percent higher than for their male counterparts.[55]

What this tells us is that Sisters need to be prepared to jump ship at least once in their careers. For some, the stint at your first (usually Stiletto) firm is like joining the Israeli army or Peace Corps—you know you have to put in some hard time for several years, but then you're outta' there. For the rest of you, it's important to address how you will feel and what to expect during the process. Basically, the progression from moving from one employer to the next parallels the following six to eight stages of a relationship.

STAGE 1: THE HONEYMOON

Is there anything more blissful than new love? Your new dish can do no wrong and everything is a refreshing and delightful adventure. The first few weeks or months at your new firm is no different. Because you have just arrived, you will be taken to lunch now and then by the partners with whom you will be working. These partners treat you like the princess that you are and are seemingly interested in your life outside of the firm. You will also spend a lot of time training and doing nonbillable, nonthinking work and usually don't stay past 5:30 on any given day (mostly because jaded midlevel associates keep telling you to leave now because *eventually, you'll be here all night*). During this brief idyllic point in time, you can't believe anyone could get a divorce and similarly, jilt this gracious firm that is paying you a lot of money to do very little.

Consequently, if you receive those nasty headhunter calls during the honeymoon (which you will start to get about 10 minutes after you begin your new job), you will be inclined to slam the phone down in their ears, refuse to take their calls, or treat them like child molesters. Keep in mind that this is a bad move, Sister, because *Stage 1* does not last forever.

STAGE 2: DISENCHANTMENT

Although it feels like a slice of heaven in the beginning, at some point within the first year or two of any relationship, little things will start to annoy you. With your lover, maybe it's his discolored front tooth, his morning breath, or his failure to replace the toilet rolls in the bathroom. With your firm, it starts off with a few late nights and then turns into three-week stints of canceling plans and consecutive all-nighters. While you were asked to observe depositions during the honeymoon, you have now been put on the indefinite twelve-hour per day due diligence routine or discovery diet. The partners who treated you with respect during your honeymoon lunches are now calling you at home at all hours of the night and tracking you down on the weekends.

At some point in either relationship, you get what Marilyn Monroe called *the itch*. You start fantasizing that there must be something else out there—that you're too good to be wasting your time with this firm. When the itch begins, you try to ignore it and hope it will go away. You can go on and on harboring, hiding, and denying this secret itch for quite awhile because you know it's the right thing to do.

When you have the itch in the beginning of *Stage 2*, you are likely to do nothing about it besides commiserate with your Bingin' and Bitchin' Buddies. The reason for staying put is generally threefold. First, unless you are Elizabeth Taylor, it looks bad to leave a relationship and jump to a new one if you've only been in it for a very short period of time (*i.e.*, under one to two years at most firms), so you may try to stick it out as long as you can bear it. Second, just as you are about to scratch the itch, your first lover does something nice, like sending you flowers or candy to make up for his inconsiderate behavior. Similarly, your firm may give you a big bonus, the partners may temporarily feel your pain and ease up on you, or you may take a vacation and for an entire week forget about how unhappy you are.

Third, and perhaps most important, is apathy. It's a pain in the neck to *get back out there* and start dating again. Likewise, the process of researching other firms, interviewing, and making decisions sends some of us reeling, not to mention the fear that we're going from the frying pan to the fire. As horrible as your current firm may be, at least you're used to the routine and how to manage the difficult personalities. Besides, the longer you hold off from scratching the itch, the more associates accumulate less senior to you—Newbies who you can dump on. Many of us may spend several years in *Stage 2* before we move on to the next stage.

STAGE 3: WINDOW SHOPPING AND EXPLORATION

Usually it takes just one straw to break the camel's back when you get to this stage. Just as your boyfriend may push you over the edge by canceling yet another date, the firm may do the same by forcing you to cancel yet another date due to work-related reasons. You start to hate your bosses, most of your colleagues, and the staff, and every work morning you wake up with an ulcer brewing in the pit of your stomach. If things are really bad, you may even feel jealous of the bag girl's job at the supermarket and surreptitiously pick up an employment application on the way out. You will finally know when you're past the point of no return when you stop complaining about jumping ship and actually do something about it. Then, you've arrived at *Stage 3*.

— Sidebar —

Sometimes, the headhunters can also precipitate this stage by telling you that the longer you stay at your firm, the more unmarketable you are becoming. The song and dance goes like this—*look, you're a 4th or 5th year already. If you wait any longer, you are going to be too expensive for any firm to hire as an associate, but not experienced enough to be hired as a partner.*

Keep the Affair Under Raps

If you are even thinking of putting yourself back on the market, you need to put the word out without letting ANYONE remotely related to your current firm know about it. It's just like dating.

Once you decide your current beau is not *the one*, you let everyone know (except him or anyone close to him) that you are available. Of course, you obviously shouldn't register for an online dating service under your current boyfriend's email address. Same holds true at the firm—bad idea to prepare cover letters and résumés on your office computer and use your office email to send the world your CV. You never know whether Big Brother is instructing the firm's computer geeks to find out who is being naughty and who is being nice. Many of us take this neurosis to a higher level by avoiding use of the office phone to talk to prospects, but in reality, as long as you shut your door when you're having these types of conversations, you should be okay.

Whether you're looking for a new boy or a new firm, you need to be discreet. Whatever you do, keep a lid on it, even from your Bingin' and Bitchin' Buddies at your current firm.

Rumors about associate departures spread like wildfire, even faster than the ones about interoffice affairs. The problem is, the world of lawyers, even in big cities like New York and L.A., can be pretty darn small. Six degrees of separation is an overstatement, and you can bet that at least one employee of your courting firm plays golf with someone at your current firm. One **Sister** told us that she was aghast when she bumped smack into her partner boss' husband (a partner at the courting firm) while she was having an interview affair. Absent special situations like that, however, most lawyers will respect your privacy as they, too, will probably one day be in your situation.

> Weirdly enough, some **Sisters** brazenly leave their résumés lying around hoping to be caught so that their bosses would be nicer to them or give them more money. (This tactic rarely works.)

Getting Back Out There

So how do you get the word out? For those of you related to the Kennedys or the Bushs, making a call to dad or his friends can't hurt. For the rest of us, it's pretty difficult to lateral into most firms absent an insider contact. So guess who now becomes your best friend? You got it—the headhunters you've been ignoring and rude to over the past several years. They are your *divorcee matchmakers* who will help you to break up with your current firm and find better love.

They will be your matchmaking saviors. Not only will they open doors that might otherwise be closed, they may also negotiate your compensation package. Best of all, they don't cost you a dime.

Sidebar

Caveat Emptor: Headhunters are like real estate brokers. Traditionally, they receive a sweet ⅓ of your annual salary at your new firm as commission, so they may have a hidden agenda when they place you at the high-paying sweatshop job. Thankfully, however, unlike real estate brokers, if you quit within three months, the headhunters must return all of their commission to the firm. This, plus their reputation in the industry (which spreads at light speed among the firms), gives them some sort of incentive to keep square pegs out of round holes.

Finding Time for The Affair

How do you go about finding new love when you spend all of your time at your current job? While some firms will agree to meet with you after hours or for breakfast, you will generally need to break away during the day for interviews. Just as if you were meeting a secret lover at a hotel at lunchtime, you must use your DESK tools to sneak out of the office for midday interviews and hope that you go undetected for a few hours at a time. The scenario typically goes something like this. You sneak out for a surreptitious lunch meeting and flirt with courting firm by telling them how great you are.

Then, you sneak back to your current office, feeling ashamed, and the guilt is further compounded as you blatantly lie about your whereabouts. If you weren't offered a job on the spot by the courting firm, you may stay extra late to make up the few hours you missed, trying to atone for your wrongdoings during that day.

Sidebar

Of course, you'll also have to perfect the party line about why you want to leave your current lover. If you are switching practices (*i.e.*, litigation to transactional) or if your current firm is going bankrupt, not a problem. However, if you are making the move for *lifestyle* reasons, you'll have to invent a reason, because no firm wants to hear that you want to work less than you currently do.

What happens when you have to interview with multiple firms or go back and revisit multiple attorneys at the courting firm? You will need a good excuse for taking so much time away from your current firm. Most of us resort to the recurring medical appointment. If your boss is male, think female-related gynecological or urological problem. Just uttering the words *cyst* or *urinary tract infection* will make him squirm in his chair, avoid eye contact, and excuse you indefinitely. While you may also use the girl-problem excuse with female bosses, you risk the chance that they have already experienced the ghastly issue and may drill you about the finer details of your ailment.

For a foolproof excuse, you may want to try the recurring dentist appointment. Assuming you don't work for a British law firm, all of the lawyers there understand the necessity of taking care of those pearly whites and the time it takes to do so. Everyone also knows that dentists don't work after 5 p.m. or on weekends. And, unlike the reoccurring doctor's appointment, nobody speculates, starts rumors, or unnecessarily worries about your health.

References from Jilted Lovers

When is the last time a guy said anything nice about a girl who dumped him? Probably never. In fact, he usually refers to her with some explicative that we can't print in this book. Whereas new boyfriends don't require referrals from old ones (and, in fact, usually don't want to know any details whatsoever about your dating escapades before them), it doesn't work that way in the job market.

Most potential employers want someone to vouch for you—a person to tell them you are in fact that shining star in the sky you profess to be. Hopefully, you have a Bingin' and Bitchin' Buddy who is senior to you that knows the scoop (and can keep a secret) who will play the role. Sometimes, the new employer asks if he can contact your old boss once they give you an offer. While it rarely happens after the offer is made, it probably serves as a litmus test to see how you would respond.

STAGE 4: THE OFFER AND SEALING THE DEAL

At some point in the *cheating* process, one of your prospects will make you an offer to join them for an ostensibly kinder, gentler practice. Perhaps you are not ready or don't have the heart to leave your first love, so you politely reject. Like a jilted lover, the new firm may continue to court you by sweetening the offer with *secret* bonuses that you can't tell the other kiddies about because it's a lockstep firm. Eventually, your current firm will commit some act that pushes you over the edge and almost as a knee-jerk reaction, you decide to run away with your new lover to escape your current one.

STAGE 5: CONFESSING YOUR AFFAIR AND THE BREAKUP

Once you have a sweet offer in your back pocket, the soap opera is far from over. You still have to break up with your current firm. You should not, however, run into your boss' office with the news until you have properly prepared to do so. Understand that as soon as you initiate the breakup, you go from being a team member to the outsider (or in hostile breakups, the enemy) and the firm may be watching you like a hawk to see what is leaving the premises. So before you drop the bomb, we would recommend gathering the fruits of your labor to take with you when you move on to greener pastures. You want all of your work product, forms, and whatever else will be helpful to you in your future employment.

Once you gather all of your goods, you will need to brace yourself for the announcement. If you have a good relationship with your direct boss, it's a good idea to rehearse the skit in your head around the lame breakup theme, *It's not you, it's me* (i.e., the new firm will provide me better opportunities for where I am now in my career). Those **Sisters** who have had less than civil relationships with their bosses, however, have probably been fantasizing about this moment for the past two years and less tactful words come to mind. No matter what the relationship, it's a good idea to avoid burning the proverbial

Sometimes, your first love will promise that things will change if only you would stick around longer, and so too may your current firm. It seems that most **Sisters** who were sucked back into the relationship at that point eventually ended it within the next year anyway.

bridge as it may come back to haunt you, particularly if you are forced to progress to *Stages 6* and *7*.

Oftentimes **Sisters** will draft a written letter stating that they are resigning. We suggest that you keep it simple and leave out any detailed explanations (and explicatives) about the firm. Hopefully, once the letter is in the hand of the powers that be, the staff can commence planning your farewell festivities with free food and booze and the undesirables won't give you any more work. Some **Sisters** report that the highpoint of their career is sending around their email farewell to the firm, which contains their forwarding address and messages that leave one and all wondering exactly what they meant, like

"Thank you for this *interesting* experience."

or

"*Some* of you make this a great place to work."

or

"I will be in touch as *time permits.*"

We specifically have heard the story of one employment firm whose unhappy associates would intentionally draft resignation letters that were so vague, they left the partners worrying that the firm would be imminently sued for something.

Now you've dropped the bomb and you're ready to flap your wings to freedom (at least temporarily). We're talking nothing matters for the next two weeks (the typical notice period unless the firm's goons escort you to the door sooner). When you come, when you leave, and what you do in between is irrelevant. Perhaps the rainmaking partners, who never acknowledged your existence, will take you to lunch and conduct an exit interview with you so that you don't bad mouth the firm after you leave (or ask you to refer them business if you're going in-house). And don't forget about the sweetest parting gift of them all—assuming you didn't exhaust your vacation days, most firms will cash you out when you leave.

STAGE 6: THE NEW HONEYMOON PERIOD

So now you're with your new dish. It's honeymoon time again. You'll probably spend the first few weeks getting to know the place and the cast of characters, and playing Lawyer Geography with everyone there. Hopefully, this will be the honeymoon that lasts a lifetime.

STAGE 7: THE RECONCILIATION

In many cases, **Sisters** sadly discover that their honeymoon with firm #2 sours just as it did with firm #1, if not worse. Perhaps there was some truth to that annoying line your mother used to use over and over again, *You won't appreciate me until I'm gone.* At this point, many **Sisters**, jaded by the entire job search process, look for salvation in the only thing they know—their first love.

> Lawyer Geography— like playing six degrees of separation with Kevin Bacon. Everyone knows someone who knows someone with whom you grew up, went to high school, college, camp, law school, etc.

With your tail between your legs, you give your old boss a call and you play noncommittal when he asks how things are going. If you had a good relationship with him and didn't send around a nasty resignation letter, perhaps he will welcome you back with open arms. If you return, you will go through a reconciliation phase that involves telling people how horrible firm #2 treated you and how you will never leave firm #1's loving arms again.

— Sidebar —

Weirdly enough, many **sisters** who went back to their first loves after anywhere from six months to a year of practicing somewhere else reported that they picked up on the exact same matters in the exact same place as where they left off (some things in law move very slowly). Therefore, it is not advised to burn, misfile, or otherwise tamper with your work product before you leave firm # 1, no matter how much you hated it there. You never know what will come back to haunt you!

STAGE 8: PUNISHMENT AND RETRIBUTION

When you get back together with an old love after a breakup, nothing can ever be the same—some wounds will not heal and perhaps you can never be trusted again after having that affair. It's the same deal when you go back to firm #1. The firm may never actually believe that you are 100% committed and loyal to the cause. Your act of jumping ship will be viewed as impulsive and childish. But the worst part is, because they have handed you a life vest by giving you back your old job, you have lost all rights to do what you do best—complain about how miserable you are to anyone at the firm.

OUR FINAL SWAN SONG

In summary, ladies of the law, we hope that if you take anything away from this book, it is the following.

The first few years of **Sisterhood** knocks even the most hardened women off balance and oftentimes the only thing that keeps us from falling flat on our LASSes is another **Sister** to lean on. Your Bingin' and Bitchin' Buddies are your lifelines in those early years, so seek them out. If you decide to leave the practice and surround yourself by non-**Sister** types, you may be surprised to find a void in your life. The wit, intelligence, acumen, and understanding that **Sisters** share as a result of the training and hazing rituals that we experience together bonds us in a way that even we are at a loss to describe.

The last (really, this is it) point we wanted to impress upon you before we depart and go back to our paying jobs is this—we recognize that much of this book is a scathing, cynical, and satirical review of what life is like as a female attorney. We hope our jaded prose has not discouraged you from pursuing your dreams and aspirations. Rather, you should recognize that the only way many of us manage to stay sane is by poking fun at the quirky behavior that consumes us in our everyday existence in this fine practice.

In other words, **Sisterhood** has its privileges. If you can keep laughing, you'll eventually learn to appreciate them.

■ ■ ■

Endnotes

[1] Good for you, reading the endnotes is key! Endnotes are typically used by lawyers to hide (and distinguish) information that will blow their client's case away or to add immaterial information that has no place in the text. We invoke the second reason here and give credit where credit is due for this statistic. *Current Glance of Women in the Law*, ABA Commission on Women in the Profession (2001).

[2] National Association of Law Placement (NALP), *Representation of Women and Attorneys of Color among Law Firm Partners — 2003*.

[3] Jonathon Glater, *Legal Research, Get me Sushi, with Footnotes*, New York Times (October 22, 2003).

[4] *Id.* (No, not Freud's id. This is just a shorthand for the last citation).

[5] Antitrust geekoids love to talk about the great claim that underlies this monopolistic system, but we have no knowledge of a lawsuit ever being brought on this basis.

[6] If you don't believe us, check out Vault.com, Crain's, American Lawyer, and our favorite whiney publication, Greedyassociates.com.

[7] Skadden, Arps, Slate, Meagher & Flom LLP is ranked among the top ten law firms in America.

[8] A recent study conducted by NALP revealed that *38%* of new associates departed from law firms within the *first three years* of employment, and *60%* of large firm associates changed jobs at least once in the first *five* years of practice. Nearly one out of five attorneys left by the second year and more than half of big firm lawyers left by the third year. More importantly, the attrition rates for women were five percent higher than for their male counterparts! The NALP Foundation, *Keeping the Keepers II: Mobility and Management of Associates* (analyzing hiring and departure data from 1998 to 2003).

[9] Karen Sisco is the smart and sexy United States Marshall in ABC's action-filled drama *Karen Sisco* (a spin-off of Elmore Loenard's novel, *Out of Sight*). She pursues dangerous fugitives from the law and must navigate her way through the dark underbelly of South Beach nightlife, as well as, the glamour and glitz of Palm Beach.

[10] This is the office simulation exercise in which lawyers are told to behave while the vacationing tourists (law students) are in town.

[11] Jared Sandberg, *Workplace Klepto Culture Squanders Key Resources,* Wall Street Journal, Career Journal.com.

[12] Jared Sandberg, *Office Copiers Cultivate Love/Hate Relationships,* Wall Street Journal, Career Journal.com.

[13] Jared Sandberg, *Ghosts of Lunches Past Haunt Office Microwaves,* Wall Street Journal, CareerJournal.com.

[14] *Id.*

[15] We know, we're being drama-queens here, but even excluding the cost of your time, you're still ahead of the game buying pre-prepared items in many cases.

[16] No, this is not a typo. A freshly cooked Costco chicken is cheaper than the raw chicken you purchase at the supermarket.

[17] In reality, no $isters do this. However, one of your authors desperately wants to impress her Italian mother-in-law who hopefully does not read endnotes, so let's keep that between us girls.

[18] Kegel is the name of a pelvic floor exercise post-prego $isters often do to strengthen pelvic muscles, or more notably, to prevent pee-pee accidents after having a baby.

[19] TheKnot.com Flash poll survey from February 2004.

[20] Ralph Gardner Jr., *Alpha Women Beta Men: Wives are Increasingly Outearning Their Husbands, But their New Financial Muscle is Causing Havoc in the Home*, New York Magazine (November 17, 2003).

[21] We are still trying to figure out when "mature age" started to mean over 30.

[22] Michelle Quist Mumford, *Guilty of Pregnancy at Large Law Firm*, Perspectives, Magazine of the ABA Commission on Women in the Profession (Spring 2003).

[23] Williams, Joan and Cynthia Thomas Calvert, *Balanced Hours: Effective Part-Time Policies for Washington Law Firms*, The Project for Attorney Retention (2002).

[24] Eldridge, Lisa Carney and Deborah Epstein Henry, *Cashing In on Part-Time*, The Bencher (American Inns of Court publication, March/April 2003).

[25] *Id.*

[26] Susan Mandel, *Firms and Family*, American Bar Association Journal, September 2003.

[27] Goldhaber, Michael D., *Part-Time Never Works: Discuss*, The National Law Journal, December 4, 2000.

[28] *See* www.lawcost.com/clifchancememo.htm for the full scoop.

[29] Dahila Lithwick, *Free the Baby Lawyers! Deprogramming the Associates at Clifford Chance*, MSN.com (October 29, 2002).

[30] Two authorities support this premise, and we thought we'd bury it in this end-note because they are so depressing. First, researchers affiliated with Johns Hopkins University found statistically significant elevations of depression in three professions, lawyers, of course, topping the list, at a rate 3.6% higher than non-lawyers. As if that isn't upsetting enough, the rate of alcoholism among lawyers is double the rate for adults generally and the divorce rate higher than any other pro-fession (most particularly pronounced among women). Patrick Schlitz, *Those Unhappy, Unhealthy Lawyers*, Notre Dame Magazine (Autumn 1999). Second, new research from the University of Texas, Houston, suggests that your job may be killing you: people who lack control over their work have a 43% greater risk of dying prematurely than other employees. Sue Shellenbarger, *The 'Chair Boogie' and Other Ways for Stressed-Out Workers to Chill Out*, Wall Street Journal (October 3, 2002).(We can only imagine that it must be even higher for lawyers given the abovementioned pressures.)

[31] Nick Wingfield, *The Rise and Fall of Web Shopping at Work*, Wall Street Journal (September 27, 2002).

[32] *Id.*

[33] *Id.*

[34] Alex Pham, *Women Take Lead in Filling Online Carts as More Pick PC's Over Shopping at Malls*, Los Angeles Times (January 7, 2004).

[35] Jared Sandberg, *Longing for a Summer Spent in your Cubicle*, Wall Street Journal, CareerJournal.com.

[36] Lawyerese for "we'll do our best, but if we fail, you have no cause of action against us."

[37] The Uniform System of Citation used for legal writing.

[38] Take the comments of the wise and legendary U.S. 9th Circuit Judge Alex Kozinski, for example, who once wrote that "a fat brief" shows that a lawyer has "a rotten case" and lacks an argument "capable of being presented in a simple, direct, persuasive fashion." Alex Kozinski, *The Wrong Stuff*, 1992 B.Y.U.Law Rev. 325, 326(1992).

[39] This is one element that determines if a contract is formed between two parties.

[40] Lawyerese for "awkward, please reword."

[41] In this television show, five gay men transform a style-deficient and cultural-deprived straight man from drab to fab with respect to fashion, food, wine, interior design, grooming, and culture.

[42] Actually, we have no personal alliances to the firm, but we graciously acknowledge the fact that once all the other big national firms got wind of the dramatic salary increases, it caused an across-the-nation increase for all associate salaries. For that, we pay our respects to the now defunct Brobeck. May it rest in peace.

[43] As an aside, one urban legend that has made its rounds was the so called *dream weekend* offered by one of the big New York City law firms, whereby all summer associates who received offers were allowed to pick a weekend outing and have the firm pay for it. Whereas most of the kids limited their *dream* to a fancy dinner or carriage ride through Central Park, one gluttonous lad flew to Paris for the weekend with his girlfriend *a la* firm. Thanks to his *chutzpah* (or maybe just a weakening economy), this firm sadly put an end to the dream.

[44] Joanna L. Krotz, *Why Women Make Better Managers*, Microsoft bCentral (www.bcentral.com/articles/krotz/150asp?LID34660)(2004).

[45] Cynthia Thomas Calvert, *Making the Most of Your Natural Talents: Negotiation Skills for Women Lawyers*, Women Lawyers Directory (www.womenlawyers.com/dealing.htm) and *Raising the Bar*, Women's Bar Assn. of District of Columbia (1999).

[46] *Id.*

[47] *Id.*

[48] *Going to the Printer*, Vault.com (February 3, 2003).

[49] *Id.*

[50] *Id.*

[51] *Id.*

[52] Kate Kelly and Shelly Branch, *Agony of the Feet: Fashion Says If the Shoe Fits, What's the Point*, Wall Street Journal (August 8, 2003).

[53] *The Many Faces of a Bankruptcy Lawyer*, Vault.com (April 7, 2003).

[54] *See supra*, The NALP Foundation.

[55] *Id.*

-Appendix A-

acronyms

A

AA—*Adulterous Affair*. A partner's extramarital transgression with a **Sister**.

ASS—*Attorney Senior Supervisors*. Senior attorneys to whom the newbies report during their training years.

B

BITCH—*Because Ibuprofen Tylenol Can't Help*. The task is so daunting that even Ibuprofen Tylenol cannot help make it better.

BBQ—*Ball Busting Ice Queens*. **Sisters** who do not pretend to be another **Sisters** friend, mentor, or champion. Their bark and bite are equally stinging.

C

CAD—*Culinary Affirmative Defense*. An excuse for why **Sisters** don't cook.

CRAPS—*Chronic Research Anxiety Phobia Syndrome*. A full-blown anxiety attack that occurs when **Sisters** are given a legal research assignment that they don't understand and don't know how to even begin.

D-Day—*Deposition Day*. The day in which depositions are taken in a major case.

DESK—*Decoy Escape Sister Kit*. The tools (purse, keys, specs, jacket, bait, and perfume) that you use to give the impression that you are working all night when you are not.

DL—*Down Low*. When you want to keep something under wraps.

EARS—*Emergency Atkins Recovery Supplies*. Carb-rich foods.

GP—*General Practitioner*. An attorney who practices a number of different areas of law, but is generally not an expert in any one practice area.

HINDS—*Hearing Impaired New Dad Syndrome*. A condition that affects new dads who become legally deaf between the hours of 10 p.m. and 7 a.m. and awake each morning with bruised shins from Sisters' ineffectual attempt to kick their butts out of bed.

IRAC—*Issue, Rule, Analysis, and Conclusion*. The draconian rule governing how one must write a legal memorandum in law school. Issue: state the issue to be presented. Rule: state the rule of law that applies. Analysis: apply the rule of law to the facts of the case. Conclusion: sum up the answer to the issue presented.

LASS—*Lawyers Ass Spread Syndrome*. Like the freshman fifteen, only it is a first year fifty and it distributes itself entirely in a **Sister's** butt as a result of spending far too much time in a desk chair.

LIE—*Law Interviewing Embellishing*. A little white lie that **Sisters'** employ to make themselves stand out during an interview.

MIA—*Missing in Action* (Devices). The electronic leash that keeps **Sisters** connected to work. These include Crackberries, cell phones, pagers, home fax machines, and email.

MUM—*Markup Madness*. Changes to an agreement.

PP—*Partner Paranoia*. A condition that affects a **Sister** within seconds of spotting a call coming in from a dreaded partner. Her heart starts racing, she sweats through her silk blouse, and she eats no less than fifteen Hershey Kisses to take the edge off this dire situation.

PTC—*Preggers Trump Card*. An excuse a pregnant **Sister** employs to get out of anything and everything.

SAD—*Summer Associate Delusion*. Wining and dining summer associates on the firm's tab.

SAHM—*Stay At Home Mommy*. A **Sister** who quits the **Sisterhood** to become a full-time mommy.

SINS—*Secret Insiders Names*. Phony names to identify a super-secret deal.

SOX—*Sarbanes-Oxley Act*. A law passed in response to the collapse of Enron and succeeding corporate scandals.

TesTy—*Testosterone Tyrant.* A member of the old boys' club who respects no one, especially women, or a slimy, slithery guy who is incapable of looking at women without seeing breasts and ass.

TTC—*Trying To Conceive.* The *trying to have a baby* phase of your life.

WMTC—*Working Mommy Trump Card.* An excuse working mommy **Sisters** employ to get out of anything and everything.

WC—*Water Closet.* The Euro way to say bathroom.

-Appendix B-

Frequently used phrases

All-Nighter Exercise Route
The route Sisters take to explore the whole office when they are pulling an all-nighter.

Anal-Retentive Disorder
Sisters become obsessed with punctuation, grammar, spelling, and even word spacing. Closely related is Sisters compulsion to tab, file, color code, and numerically stamp anything that lands on her desk, including the Chinese takeout menu. Before long, this compulsion extends to organizing everything in a Sister's world.

Appreciating the Queen Beast
Generating revenues on behalf of Sister's employers.

Bathroom Route
The route to and from the bathroom.

Beauty Contest

A potential deep-pocket client is treated to over-the-top PowerPoint presentations and dog and pony shows by several different firms that promise to cure all of their company's ills on a shoestring budget.

Blackberry

A traveling email device.

Blackline

A word processing program that shows each and every change made to a document.

Bingin' and Bitchin'

The art of complaining and blowing off steam with a **Sister's** closest confidants.

Brain Drain

A pregnant **Sister** experiences early Alzheimer's. The symptoms include fatigue, highly emotional tirades, and healthier skin.

Brothers-in-Law Male lawyers.

Cause and Effect Disorder

A belief that everything has to happen for a distinct reason, which must be supported by clear and convincing evidence.

Closing

Consummation of a deal.

Country Club Prison

The printers' office that is fully equipped with showers, all the food a Sister can eat, and other amenities to accommodate *lock-ins until you're done* sessions.

Crackberry

See *Blackberry*.

Cross-Trainers

See *General Practitioners*.

Delegation Deficit Disorder

A condition also known as micromanaging. It usually first develops when a paralegal, secretary, or junior associate to whom a Sister delegates work makes a small blunder, leading the Sister to never again delegate anything to anyone without worrying and obsessing that they will screw it up.

Discovery

A formal investigation of the facts of a case that is conducted before trial. It allows one party to question the other party or obtain documents or other evidence that is reasonably calculated to lead to the discovery of admissible evidence.

Dog and Pony Parade Route

The scenic tour of a **Sister's** office. It typically includes the most impressive conference rooms and corner offices.

Due Diligence

Gathering enough information about a client and the other company in order to structure the deal and fine-tune the terms and conditions of the contract underlying the deal.

Escape from Alcatraz Route

The shortest and most discrete route from a **Sister's** workspace to the elevator/entranceway, measured in time and distance.

Frog

The Bugaboo Frog, a see-and-be-seen, over-priced status stroller.

Gross Rationalization Disorder

A condition in which **Sisters** rationalize anything they do, no matter how imprudent or stupid, because they have very little time to do it themselves.

| Hasta La Vista Litigation |

Opposing counsel writes hateful and intolerable accusatory letters personalizing the dispute as if the **Sister** committed the wrong herself.

| It's Not Fair Litigation |

Parties base an entire lawsuit on the mistaken belief that certain conduct is unfair, and therefore, in their "legal expertise," is unlawful.

| Kvetching |

A Yiddish word for complaining.

| Learn and Burn Method |

A training method in which a **Sister** is given limited or no direction at all. She is handed a client file and told to take care of it.

| Library Route |

The routes from your office to the library.

| Mary Janes |

Government gigs.

| Me and My Shadow Method |

A training method in which senior attorneys run the show and allow **Sisters**-in-training to observe.

Multitasking Madness Disorder

A condition in which **Sisters** juggle an overwhelming number of personal and professional demands each and everyday.

Orthopedic Shoes

In-house counsel gig.

Paperectomy

The removal of paper stuck in a copier, fax, or other office machine.

Pee-Pee Predicament

The dilemma that happens when a **Sister** must decide whether to abort a mission to the bathroom when someone for whom she works is in there.

Perfection Disorder

A condition in which a **Sister**, after getting reamed by a client or boss on a wholly insignificant mistake, vows to be 200% perfect forever.

Platform Heels

The mid-size law firm.

Player's List

All the contact information for all the warm bodies working on a Deal.

Possessed State

Pregnant.

Post-Close/Post-Filing Euphoria Disorder

A condition that occurs after a big deal closes or a big motion is filed with the court. Characterized by an overwhelming feeling of happiness and invincibility, immediately followed by a complete shutdown of total uselessness and laziness.

Printing Party

The event that occurs when a prospectus is near completion, in which the lawyers, bankers, and senior management of the parties hammer out all the fine details of the Deal.

Prospectus

A lengthy document that sets forth certain disclosures for public corporations before they take some sort of material action that will affect the company.

Red Herring

Copies of the preliminary prospectus.

Redline

Changes to a document made by hand in red ink.

Rollerblades

Hang-a-Shingle shop.

Scorch the Earth Litigation

A litigation technique in which one party prepares a complaint by throwing every cause of action imaginable against the wall and seeing what will stick.

Shephardizing

Checking out the history of legal authority to make sure it is still good law.

Shielding

Protecting summer associates from the wrath of certain partners.

Shuga Daddy

Prince Charming with lots and lots of *moola* so a Sister never has to work again.

Shuga Mama

An endearing term for a Sister who wears the pants in the family because she earns more money than her hubby.

Ski Boots

Specialized boutique law firm.

Socializing the Beast

Interacting with others in the legal world.

Specialist

An attorney who practices one area of the law.

Spinning Shoes

See *Specialist*.

Spots Gene

A gene which enables men to bond with their brethren over anything sports-related.

Stilletos

The full-service law firm.

Subpoenas

A legal instrument that allows one party to request information from another person.

Summary Judgment Motion

A motion made by a party requesting that the Court dismiss a lawsuit because the causes of actions are not actionable as a matter of law.

Term Sheet

The basic elements of an agreement in a deal usually presented in a two-columned list with each issue on the left and how it will be resolved on the right.

Time is Money Disorder

A condition that forces a **Sister** to make every nonbillable minute something productive.

Toil Away in Isolation Method

A training technique in which senior attorneys give new attorneys no direction at all, and at the same time allow them free reign to do everything.

Understanding the Beast Within

The methods in which a **Sister** learns her trade.

U-Turn

When a **Sister** aborts a mission (you turn) to the bathroom the second she sees someone for whom she is working in there.

Wearing the Cute Pants in the Family

Salvaging a **Sister's** husband's ego because she earns more money than he does.

White Shoe Litigation

A litigation method in which all counsel are pleasant and even friendly with each other and respect the other sides' differing positions. Requests and favors are always granted and time frames are always extended indefinitely. No hate mail or threats are ever exchanged. After each side has built up their case, the sides seek resolution amicably or try the case.

Index

About the Authors

Lisa G. Sherman, Esq. graduated from the University of Rochester in 1990 with a Bachelors of Arts degree in Economics and Political Science. Surrounded by a family full of physicians (all of whom hated lawyers) and deathly afraid of the sight of blood, she took refuge in law school.

Lured by the prospect of cheap Budweiser beer, Ms. Sherman journeyed west to Washington University School of Law in St. Louis, Missouri. After three years of watching her parents (native Brooklyn, New Yorkers), haggle with the mild-mannered mid-westerners over the price of everything they bought her, and attending a few classes along the way, she graduated in 1993. Much to her own surprise, she was awarded an American Jurisprudence Award in Trial Advocacy (most likely, for her ability to persuasively talk herself out of any situation).

After showing up to an interview with her leg in a cast, she was offered a position with two Washington University alumni at one of the most prestigious law firms in Nevada, practicing labor and employment law, representing management. Knowing no one and absolutely nothing about gambling, prostitution, or, for that matter, labor and employment law, Ms. Sherman moved to Sin city after graduation.

After taking the Nevada Bar, Ms. Sherman met her Prince Charming, who was attending medical school in Los Angeles, California. Following nine months of commuting on Southwest Airlines, Mr. Right proposed to Ms. Sherman, and she demonstrated her love for him by moving to Los Angeles, suffering through the infamous California Bar Exam, marrying him (not to mention taking his last name), and rooting for the Los Angeles Dodgers.

Ms. Sherman has practiced labor and employment law ever since graduation, having done her time at the nation's largest labor and employment firm, two highly prestigious boutique law firms in California and Nevada, and before writing this book, contracting on her own. She has had great success as a litigator representing her clients in court and before administrative agencies and arbitration panels. Devoting much of her practice to defending employers and high-level employees accused of sexual harassment, she has heard and seen it all from Lewinskyesque dresses to consensual sexual encounters turned "fatal attraction" at strip joints, sweat shops, restaurants, and yes—even convalescent homes!

Aside from her busy law practice, raising two princesses (ages 3 and 5), and living the life of a weekend sports widow and doctor's wife, she has published a number of articles on various labor and employment law issues. Most notably, she authored, "*Exempt or Not Exempt under the Administrative Exemption of the Fair Labor Standards Act—That is the Question,*" 11 The Labor Lawyer 209 (1995); "*The New Legal Challenge to Employee Participation,*" 45 Labor Law Journal 1 (1994); "*Sexually Provocative Dress Code May Result in Liability,*" Nevada Labor

Letter, Vol II, No. 5, May 1994; *"Managing Leaves of Absence and Controlling Fraud,"* Personnel Law Update Seminar, Spring 1994; and *"Fraternization and Dating Policies: May Employers Regulate Matters of the Heart?"* 8 Personnel Law Update 12 (1993).

■ ■ ■

Deborah L. Turchiano, Esq. graduated with a degree in labor Relations from Cornell University and a mission to play with the big bad boys on Wall Street. After becoming a casualty of the early 90's investment banking firm reductions-in-force, Ms. Turchiano decided to take refuge in law school, a place where you couldn't get laid off for at least three years. Armed with her sunscreen and "y'alls", Ms. Turchiano headed south to attend the University of Florida College of Law, where she somehow managed to book a couple of classes, attend a lot of Gator games, and finally graduated in 1993. Prior to graduating, she was a summer associate for three of the largest law firms in the country in Atlanta and New York, where she was deluded into thinking that billing 15 hours a week, usually on *pro bono* matters, while taking 2 hour lunches only at the Zagat's top 50 was the paradigm of working at a big firm.

After graduation, Ms. Turchiano began her legal career clerking for the Honorable Susan H. Black on the Eleventh Circuit Court of Appeals. She then spent seven years grinding away as a captive of a Wall Street law firm. There, she specialized in transactional employment law and executive compensation with an emphasis on tax and securities law. During that time, she met a guy, now her husband, who didn't care that she had to cancel 90% of their dates due to work, with the remaining 10% of the dates occurring at or after 11 p.m. when she left the office.

Ms. Turchiano currently practices at an executive compensation consulting firm, where she negotiates employment contracts and compensation arrangements for Fortune 500 executives and keeps such executives out of Enron-like trouble. In her "spare" time, Ms. Turchiano has published a number of articles and chapters such as, *Chapter 8: Perquisites,* Executive Compensation and Benefits Handbook, *BNA Publications* (2002), *IRS Changes Rules through Field Service Advice—This Time on FICA and ESPP,* Journal of Taxation of Employee Benefits, RIA Group Publishing (January/February 2000), *The New Qualified Plan Minimum Distribution Rules,* The New York Law Journal (Winter, 1996), *Chapter 12: Negotiating and Drafting Employment Agreements,* Executive Compensation: The Professional's Guide to Current Issues & Practices (2004), and *Chapter 15: Executive Compensation as a Corporate Governance Issue,* Corporate Governance (to be released 2004).

Ms. Turchiano and her husband (an engineer, because someone has to do long division) live in New York City with their one-year-old daughter and yellow lab—the mandatory Upper West Side accessories.

■ ■ ■

Jill R. Schecter, Esq. attended the University of California, Berkeley, where she graduated Phi Beta Kappa with a major (benefiting the university infamous for the free speech movement) in Rhetoric. Armed with expertise in argument-for-argument's sake and oral poetry recitation skills, she attended law school at the University of California, Los Angeles. By 1993, she had collected a law degree, a wonderful husband, and a nasty black cat.

After graduation, Ms. Schecter clerked for the Honorable Arthur L. Alarcon of the Ninth Circuit Court of Appeals until the fall of 1995, and also enjoyed a successful construction litigation practice with a boutique firm in Los Angeles. It was there she developed proficiency in walking through a construction zone in a hardhat and heels.

Ms. Schecter and her husband, a litigation partner at a Los Angeles-based megafirm, are raising three daughter, ages 8, 5, and 1, who already show remarkable strength in the art of persuasion.

■ ■ ■

You can contact the authors at **sistersinlaw2004@yahoo.com.**